MW00807941

PRACTICAL DRESSAGE MANUAL

Bengt Ljungquist

PRACTICAL DRESSAGE MANUAL

BENGT LJUNGQUIST

Half Halt Press, Inc.

Boonsboro, Maryland

FOREWORD

Colonel Bengt Ljungquist contributed a great many things to Dressage in the United States in the short span of time that he was here. Most important of all perhaps were the following four which will be of lasting value.

The United States Equestrian Team Dressage Clinics which he held throughout the country brought advanced dressage within the reach of everyone. At last, they had a chance to both see and be seen.

The Dressage Judging Clinics which he held nationwide enabled the entire dressage community to gain an understanding and a "standard" for what is "good" and what is "insufficient."

His team captured the Bronze Medal at the 1976 Montreal Olympics. This gave the dressage community "pride." We had beaten the Russians at one of their favorite sports. We were only 37 points behind the second place Swiss.

Last, but perhaps most important of all, he wrote this book, giving American a reliable dressage text, written in English for Americans by a person who fully understood both the Americans and their horses.

CLARENCE W. EDMONDS
Colonel USAF (Retired)

PREFACE

THE aim of this noble and useful art is solely to make horses supple, relaxed, flexible, compliant and obedient and to lower the quarters, without all of which a horse—whether he be meant for military service, hunting or dressage—will be neither comfortable in his movements nor pleasureable to ride." (de la Gueriniere 1688-1751).

Though variations of style do occur, the main principles of dressage are eternal.

There are many good books on riding to help the rider to obtain or at least approach the above quoted aim. Most of them are very comprehensive, covering everything from the training of a young horse, stable management, grooming, feeding, bitting and saddlery, to the discussion of equine diseases and veterinary medicine.

This manual has been compiled as a guide for the competitive dressage rider and is dedicated to the basic training of the horse and its development up to the highest level, the Grand Prix test. It is written from the judge's point of view, explaining the proper execution and requirements of dressage movements and pointing out common faults the rider should recognize and overcome. This does not mean that this book is directed only to competitive riders. As the basic training of the horse is the same for all horses, for whatever purpose the rider wants to use the horse, the book could be useful to all riders. Most of the definitions used, are

7

taken from the FEI (Fédération Equestre Internationale) Rule-book and AHSA Notes on Dressage.

The motto is: *slow and steady*. There is no instant dressage. One should count in years, not days. It is patient daily work which pays off in the long run. A rider who does not have this patience and feels inclined to resort to special equipment, will never make a truly schooled horse. Proper equipment for schooling consists of a plain snaffle with a thick bit, a saddle and a whip. There is an old proverb which should be painted in the barn or in the indoor arena as a reminder:

"Where art ends, violence begins."

CONTENTS

Chapter I

THE COLLECTIVE MARKS

GENERAL IMPRESSIONS

PACES, IMPULSION, SUBMISSION, POSITION, SEAT OF THE RIDER AND CORRECT USE OF THE AIDS

The General Impressions are the basis for valuation of every single movement, as they express the ageless ideals of equitation. These Collective Marks or General Impressions are found in the end of every AHSA and FEI test. They enable the judge to give points to the horse for his natural ability or paces, for his impulsion, for his suppleness, obedience and submission throughout the test as a score separate from that given for specific movements. The rider also receives a score for the correctness and effectiveness of his position and aids. Ideally, the horse should move in a free and regular pace with impulsion and suppleness. The rider must sit correctly and be able to communicate with his mount.

PACES*

This is the first of the General Impression scores and the most important one at the lower levels. Good natural gaits are essential for a young dressage prospect.

Some definitions useful to the discussion of paces:

Rhythm is the regularity of footfall or period of footfall (in the walk: 1-2-3-4, 1-2-3-4; in the trot: 1-2, 1-2; in the canter: 1-2-3, 1-2-3).

---

* Note: The paces will be further dealt with in connection with the training of the horse.

11

Tempo is the speed measured in meters per minute.

Cadence is the rhythm plus impulsion which gives the pace an extra quality and is expressed by an energetic lifting of the feet from the ground.

The pure gaits are highly rewarded. A horse with a poor walk, trot or canter (i.e. ambling walk, irregular trot, four beat canter) can never get a good score. It is therefore necessary when you are looking for a dressage horse, that you select one with *three* good paces.

It is easy to be charmed by one pace, a beautiful trot for instance. *All three paces* must be acceptable. Having one poor pace is a great handicap, which in close competition can never be counterbalanced by the other two paces, even if they are very good.

The paces should be free and regular. The freedom is manifested in the way the shoulders of the horse swing forward and back. The regularity is shown by the even rhythm of the strides or steps of each gait.

In all paces the horse must be straight when moving along a straight line. On a curved line he should adjust the bend of the body to the curvature of the line he follows. The hind legs should follow in the track of the forelegs.

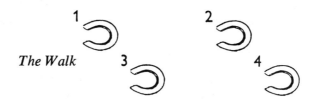

The Footfall at Walk

The walk is a pace of four time. It should always be energetic with a good drive, relaxed and unconstrained.

It is at the walk that the imperfections of dressage are most evident. This is also the reason why a horse should not be asked to accept the bit at the walk in the early stage of his training.

12

Collection before he is ready will not only spoil the collected walk, but the medium and extended walk as well. The following walks are recognized: collected, medium, extended and free.

Collected Walk

The horse, remaining on the bit, moves resolutely forward with his neck raised and arched. The head approaches the vertical position, light contact with the mouth being maintained. The hind legs are engaged, with good hock action. The pace should remain marching and vigorous, the legs being placed in regular sequence. Each step covers less ground and is higher than at medium walk because all the joints bend more markedly. The hind feet touch the ground behind or in the footprints of the forefeet. In order not to become hurried or irregular, the collected walk is shorter than the medium walk, although showing greater activity.

JOHN WINNETT   *Collected Walk*

13

Medium Walk*

The medium walk is a free, regular and unconstrained walk of moderate extension. The horse, remaining on the bit, walks energetically but calmly, with even and determined steps, the hind feet touching the ground in front of the footprints of the forefeet. The rider maintains a light but steady contact with the mouth.

Extended Walk

The horse covers as much ground as possible, without haste and without losing the regularity of his steps. The hind feet touch the ground clearly in front of the footprints of the fore-feet. The rider allows the horse to stretch out his head and neck without, however, losing contact with the mouth. He should nod slightly forward, not upward.

Free Walk

The free walk is a pace of relaxation in which the horse is allowed complete freedom to lower and stretch out his head and neck.

A mental and physical relaxation should characterize this pace. Though relaxed, the horse should maintain an energetic ground covering attitude. Remember: to relax does not mean to collapse. The longer the strides, the better. The horse must step over, the hind feet touching the ground in front of the footprints of the forefeet.

It is easy to ruin the walk by pushing the horse together too soon. Ride on minimum contact, just enough so that you can guide him.

You should always urge the horse forward into an energetic walk by driving with one leg at the time. Try to feel the action and timing of the horse's legs. The correct time to squeeze with your lower leg is when the corresponding hind foot goes up in the air. This happens immediately after the horse brings the diagonal shoulder forward. For instance, on the right rein, drive with your right leg when the horse's left foreleg touches

---

* Working walk is introduced in AHSA tests. Working walk is about the same as medium walk.

14

KAY MEREDITH   *Medium Walk*

KAY MEREDITH   *Extended Walk*

15

Free Walk

the ground. Be careful and don't be too ambitious, making the walk hurried.

An ambling walk (the horse moves the legs on the same side at the same time) is often difficult to cure. When it happens, move the horse a couple of strides sideways with your leg, relax your own hands and push forward. Work up- and down-hill is also helpful.

The Trot

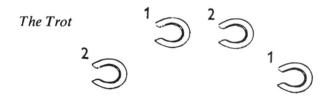

The Footfall at Trot

16

The trot is a pace of two times when the legs move in alternate diagonal pairs (near fore and off hind and vice versa) separated by a moment of suspension. It should be free, active, elastic and regular. The regularity can be broken if the foreleg touches ground before the diagonal hind leg (the hurried foreleg) or if the hindleg touches ground before the diagonal foreleg (the hasty hind leg).

The quality of the trot is judged on the regularity and elasticity of the steps and the maintenance of a steady rhythm and natural balance, all of which must originate from a supple back and well engaged hindquarters.

The following trots are recognized: collected, working, medium and extended.

The length of the strides and elevation of the steps make the main difference between these types of trot and not the speed at which the horse travels.

LINDA ZANG   *Collected Trot*

17

JOHN WINNETT

DOROTHY MORKIS   *Collected Trot*

18

Collected Trot

The horse, remaining on the bit, moves forward with his neck raised and arched. The hocks, being well engaged, maintain an energetic impulsion, thus enabling the shoulders to move with greater ease in any direction. The horse's steps are shorter than in the other trots, but he is lighter and more mobile.

The collected trot is executed sitting.

Working Trot

This is a pace between the medium and the collected trot in which a horse, not yet ready or trained for collected movements, shows himself properly balanced and, with a supple poll, remaining on the bit, goes forward with even, elastic steps and good hock action.

LENDON GRAY   *Working Trot—Young horse*
*The horse is lowering and lengthening his neck, stretching
into the bit in a relaxed way*

19

HILDA GURNEY   *Working Trot—Mature Horse*
Power and Energy
The poll, however, should be the highest point

ELIZABETH LEWIS   *Working Trot—Mature Horse*
Relaxation and Harmony

Good hock action does not mean that lowering the quarters is a required quality of the working trot; it only underlines the importance of an impulsion which originates in the activity of the quarters.

This is the ideal working trot. A young or untrained horse, however, cannot fulfill these requirements. For such a horse, the working trot is the pace at which he can best carry his rider and himself without any special strain. However, a distinct two-beat rhythm, neither sluggish nor hasty, must be present in the working trot. From this pace the medium trot and the collected trot are developed.

The working trot is executed sitting or rising. At change of rein across the diagonal the change of posting diagonal should be made when crossing the centerline.

Medium Trot

This is a pace between the working and the extended trot, but more *round* than the latter. The horse goes forward with free and moderately extended steps and an obvious impulsion from

LENDON GRAY   *Medium Trot*
Ideal frame, impulsion and relaxation

the hindquarters. The rider allows the horse, remaining on the bit, to carry his head a little more in front of the vertical than at the collected and at the working trot, and allows him at the same time to lower his head and neck slightly. The steps should be even, and the whole movement balanced and unconstrained.

A good medium trot is not easy to develop and perform. It becomes either too feeble (lack of hock action, freedom of shoulders and balance) or too powerful (resembling the extended trot). Sometimes it is an irregular running trot with short steps and without the elasticity coming from a supple back.

Extended Trot

The horse covers as much ground as possible. Maintaining the same rhythm, he lengthens his steps to the utmost, the result of great impulsion from the hindquarters. The rider allows the horse, remaining on the bit, to lower and extend his neck in order to

LINDA ZANG

Extended Trot
On this picture the nose should be positioned slightly more forward and the neck slightly lowered so that the poll remains as the highest point

22

Extended Trot

prevent his action from becoming higher. The upper outline of the neck approaches the horizontal line, the nose being in front of the vertical line. *The forefeet should touch the ground on the spot toward which they are pointing.* The hind legs reach forward without pushing backwards.

The transition into extended trot should be smooth, not explosive, and the transition back to hand must likewise be smooth. If the horse is not allowed to lower and lengthen his neck slightly he cannot lengthen his strides.

If the head is too high, the shoulders are locked, the movements of the forelegs too high (flicking of the forelegs), the hind legs drag and the shin-bones of the hind legs are not parallel with those of the foreleg. A running trot with short steps can never be scored as sufficient. An extended trot with the horse on his forehand "boring into the bit" and with dragging hindquarters is likewise incorrect.

The medium and extended trots are executed sitting or rising. When changing the rein at extended, rising trot, the change of the posting diagonal should be made upon the return to the track.

In the FEI tests, all trot work is executed sitting.

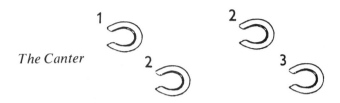

The Canter

The Footfall at Canter, Right Lead

Canter is a pace of three time. At the canter to the right, for instance, the footfall is as follows: 1) left hind, 2) left diagonal (simultaneously left fore and right hind), 3) right fore, followed by a moment of suspension with all four feet in the air before the next stride begins.

Ideally, the canter is straight, light and united, with free mobile shoulders and active quarters. Canter in four time or disunited is a grave fault. The four-beat canter occurs when the hind leg touches the ground before the corresponding diagonal foreleg. The four-beat canter is often caused when the rider has collected the horse too soon, generally with a lack of engagement of the hindquarters. If a tendency toward four-beat canter is evident, the horse should be ridden freely forward.

The canter is disunited if the front legs are on the right lead and the hind legs on the left lead, or vice versa.

The following canters are recognized: collected, working, medium and extended.

The length of the strides, not the speed at which the horse travels, makes the difference between these types of canter.

Collected Canter

The horse, remaining on the bit, moves forward with his neck raised and arched. The collected canter is marked by the lightness of the forehand and the engagement of the hindquarters: i.e. supple, free and mobile shoulders and very active quarters. The

24

horse's strides are shorter than at the other canters, but he is lighter and more mobile.

Make sure that the quarters are very active. The collected canter is not created simply by riding slower.

Working Canter

This is a pace between the collected and the medium canter in which a horse, not yet trained or ready for collected movements, shows himself properly balanced and, while remaining on the bit, goes forward with even, light and cadenced strides and good hock action.

Good hock action does not mean that collection is a required quality of the working canter; it only underlines the importance of an impulsion which originates in the activity of the quarters.

For the untrained horse the working canter is the pace in which he can best carry his rider and himself without any special strain. However, each stride of the working canter must contain a clean three-beat rhythm followed by a distinct moment of suspension without sluggishness or haste. From this pace the medium and the collected canters are developed.

LINDA ZANG   *Collected Canter*

25

Medium Canter

This is a pace between the working and the extended canter. The horse goes forward with free, balanced and moderately extended strides and with obvious impulsion from the hindquarters. The rider allows the horse, remaining on the bit, to carry his head a little more in front of the vertical than at the collected and the working canter, and allows him at the same time to lower his head and neck slightly. The strides should be long and even and the whole movement balanced and unconstrained.

The medium canter should give an impression of relaxation and roundness. This pace, like the medium trot, often becomes either too slack (lack of hock action) or too powerful, sometimes prejudicial to calmness and balance.

KAY MEREDITH   *Extended Canter*

26

Extended Canter

The horse covers as much ground as possible. Maintaining the same rhythm, he lengthens his strides to the utmost, without losing any of his calmness and lightness, the result of great impulsion from the hindquarters. The rider allows the horse, remaining on the bit, to lower and extend his head and neck, the tip of his nose pointing more or less forward.

A marked lengthening of every single stride should characterize this pace. An increased frequency of short strides is a grave fault.

IMPULSION

Impulsion is defined in the FEI tests as follows: desire to move forward, elasticity of the steps, suppleness of the back and engagement of the hindquarters.

Impulsion originates in the powerful thrust of the haunches. Only the vibrating back enables the rider to sit in a supple position. This freshness, liveliness and activity (the German expression is "Schwung") must be under control. A running trot or a fast canter with short strides are not a manifestation of impulsion. Impulsion gives the horse the desired touch of brilliance.

Impulsion must be developed. *Suppleness comes first.* Without suppleness and obedience to the rider's aids, there can be no impulsion. When the horse's muscle development and the degree of suppleness allow him to bring his haunches under him, he can achieve impulsion. That is the reason why, in the lower level tests, "willingness to go forward" in the Collective Marks is substituted for "impulsion."

Lack of impulsion can be revealed, for instance, in a backward tendency at halts, turns on the forehand and half-turns on the haunches (half-pirouettes) and at lateral movements (not fluid or forward enough).

SUBMISSION

Submission does not mean a truckling subservience, but an obedience revealing its presence by constant attention, willingness and confidence in the whole behaviour of the horse, as well as by the harmony, lightness and ease he displays in the execution of the different movements. The degree of submission is also manifested by the way the horse accepts the bridle; either with a light contact and a supple poll, or with resistance to, or evasion of, the rider's hand, being either above or behind the bit respectively. He should bend willingly to both sides in the same way, and immediately respond to the rider's aids.

Putting out the tongue, keeping it above the bit or drawing it up altogether, as well as grinding teeth and swishing the tail are generally signs of nervousness, tenseness or resistance on the part of the horse. These faults must be taken into account by the judges in their marks for the movement concerned, as well as in the collective mark for submission.

In connection with submission the expressions "on the bit," "acceptance of the bit," "above" or "behind" the bit are used.

In the FEI Rules a horse is said to be "on the bit" when the hocks are correctly placed; when the neck is more or less raised and arched according to the stage of training and the extension and collection of the pace; and when he accepts the bridle with a light contact and submissiveness throughout. The head should remain in a steady position, as a rule slightly in front of the vertical, with a supple poll at the highest point of the neck. *No resistance* should be offered to the rider.

When the horse is on the bit he is put to the aids. The rider must have the feel that the horse thinks forward, even at the halt. He should move with a supple back, show no resistance at transitions, flexions or bendings.

"Acceptance of the bit" can be considered as a lower degree of "being on the bit." A young horse should accept the bit, which means that he keeps it quietly in his mouth, does not spit it out or play with it with his tongue, or put the tongue above the bit.

The desired elastic contact with the horse's mouth is broken when the horse is "above" or "behind" the bit.

28

When the horse is "above the bit," the muscles of his neck, back and hindquarters are tense. The nose (head) is too high or stretched forward too much. The effect of the reins stops in the neck. It does not go through the body and the horse does not come off the ground with his hind feet.

When the horse is "behind the bit" (the hardest to correct of these faults), he escapes the bit completely and the rider has *no contact at all*. The remedy is to push him forward on to the bit by use of the legs. Behind the bit can sometimes be hard to recognize. For instance, it is possible for a horse to be "behind the bit" even though his neck is arched and the forehead is either on the vertical or slightly in front of it. This is the case when the rider feels that the horse does not go *willingly forward* or if he cannot *lengthen the neck of the horse.*

If you are standing on a bridge across a stream and let a piece of wood attached to a string float on the water, you feel a *gentle, soft* pull in your hand. This is the contact you must establish with the horse's mouth if you are looking for the truth. Otherwise you will never be able to lengthen the neck and therefore never be able to push your horse forward ino longer active strides. If he nods his head a little upward instead of forward, he is not honestly on the bit and the contact is not correct.

On the other hand, the head of the horse can sometimes be lowered so much that the nose comes behind the vertical. This sometimes happens with the young horse to make it easier for him to arch his back and carry the rider's weight, or with an old "criminal" who must be brought to complete submission. Consequently the horse can be on the bit (accepting the bit), but be behind the vertical. He is *not* behind the bit. There is no danger in lowering his head if he maintains the contact and stretches into the bit. It is no problem to elevate the head later on. But if he comes behind the bit, the rider will be in trouble.

For how to correct horses above or behind the bit, see Chapter VII.

29

The perfectly seated rider does not always get a good mark. He must be able to communicate with his horse and present it in a favourable way. What good is elegance if the horse is not moving well?

Riding with both hands is obligatory at all international dressage tests published by the FEI. However, when leaving the arena at a walk on a long rein, after having finished his performance, the rider may, at his own discretion, ride with only one hand.

The use of the voice in any way whatsoever, or clicking the tongue once or repeatedly, is a serious fault, involving deduction of at least two marks from that which would otherwise have been awarded for the movement where this occurred.

Observe!

The basis for the judge's estimation of your ride is not solely the precision of the movement (formal correctness), but *partly* the degree of freedom, evenness, regularity, rhythm (cadence) and impulsion that characterizes the paces; *partly* the degree of lightness, suppleness, ease, balance and harmony that characterizes the cooperation between horse and rider in executing the movements.

The precision adds to your scores and is, of course, very important, but a poor mover is always handicapped in comparison to a good mover, however precise his movements are. The rhythmical forward movement should never be sacrificed for a minute detail of accuracy.

However, once your horse is supple and obedient you can increase your scores considerably by riding with precision. Be careful to start and finish the movements at the prescribed marker; conscientiously ride the phase of the pace required (working, medium, extended, collected), perform the figures in the correct size; be meticulous in performing the required number of strides in the rein-back and piaffer as well as the correct number of flying changes.

The General Impressions set the goal of dressage riding.

Let us now see how we can strive for it.

30

Chapter II

THE SEAT • THE AIDS

THE SEAT

Only from a correct seat can a rider give correct aids and influence his horse in a correct way.

A firm position of the middle part of the body must be obtained. The rider should sit in the horse, not on top of it. The two seatbones and the crotch form a triangle ($\triangle$) on which the rider sits. All influence originates from this basis. The seat is of great importance because only the rider who understands how to contract and relax his loin muscles at the right moment is able to influence his horse correctly. The rider must also be able to use his legs and hands without moving this basis.

The seat is a question of balance. Longeing and riding without stirrups must therefore be performed until the rider can sit relaxed without squeezing with the lower legs in order to remain in the saddle.

The thighs and the knees are kept flat and steady to the saddle, the kneecaps pointing forward. The lower legs (the inside of your legs, not the back of your calves, towards the horse) are stretched downward without tension and with as much contact as the position of the knee permits. This contact should be light. The feet should be almost parallel to the horse, the toes not pointing outward. The inside part of the heel must be the lowest part of the body. Watching the rider from the side, one should see a little of the sole of the boot. By lowering the heel, the knee is lowered at the same time. The lower leg should always be used with a lowered heel, thus giving firmness and strength to the leg.

31

You must bear down on the heel. If the knees are drawn up, the buttocks are pushed backwards, resulting in the armchair-seat.

At halts and riding straight forward, the legs are kept immediately behind the girth to influence the hindquarters. If you want to influence the forehand, for instance while bending the horse, your lower leg is moved to a position *on* the girth. The

ELIZABETH LEWIS   *The Seat*

The rider erect and relaxed. As illustrated on the pictures, the shoulders, hip and heel must be on the same vertical line. There should be a straight line from the elbow to the bit. The rider should sit in the middle of the saddle (the deepest part of the saddle).

32

The Seat

lower leg should never squeeze constantly. The horse then becomes dead to the legs. Keep your lower leg quiet and increase the pressure when necessary. If a squeeze does not work, loosen your lower leg and give the horse a short, sharp kick. After the kick, your leg must remain close to the horse and not bounce out again. Your hands must remain quiet. If necessary, support the leg by using the whip behind the boot. As the obedience of the horse gradually develops, refine your aids until you can "whisper" to your horse, meaning that the horse will respond immediately to the slightest squeeze of your legs.

The stirrups are there for the posting trot. At the sitting trot they should never carry the weight of the rider. The length of the leathers is correct if you can pick up the stirrups by lifting your toes, the heel remaining in its low position. Consequently the sole of your boots should be higher than the heel.

33

The upper part of the body should be relaxed, free and erect, head and neck carried in a natural way without tension in the neck. Draw your chin back slightly and do not nod your head in the rhythm of the horse's movements. Look forward, never down, and look proud as if you own the whole world.

The shoulders should be lowered and pulled slightly backward so that the chest gets a natural arch. Tension generally starts in the shoulders. If you feel tense, relax your shoulders by rolling them backward and then let them drop down.

The back should be straight without tension, neither rounded nor hollow, the hipjoints supple.

The upper arms hang down relaxed, keeping a very light contact with the upper body. The lower arms, hands and reins form a straight line to the bit.

POSITION OF THE HANDS
HOLDING THE REINS

Keep your hands a little above the withers, thumb up and flat towards the reins. Close your fists without cramping them. If you turn your hands with the nails down and the knuckles up, you lose the elasticity of your rein and create a tension which goes up to the shoulders, making the elbows come out. The hands should be fairly close to each other, so that you frame the neck of the horse with your reins.

Right—Thumbs Up and Flat, Wrists Straight

34

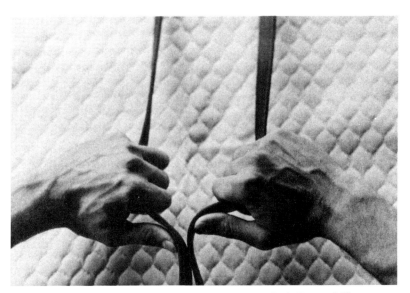

Wrong—Palms Down and Wrists Broken Out Which Causes Stiffness

Wrong—Wrists Broken Inward

35

Your hands must be:

steady .... so that you can keep them in the position you want, independent of the rest of the body,

soft .... so that you can gradually increase and decrease the influence of the bit,

sensitive .... so that you can immediately feel the slightest change of contact,

flexible ..... so that you can follow the natural movements of the horse's head.

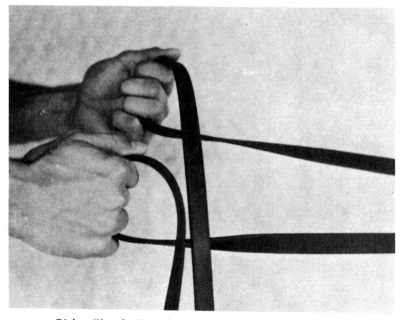

Right—Thumbs Up and Flat; Left Hand Is Raised in Order to Show Position of Reins Through the Fingers

---

NOTE: If your work has been correct in the snaffle no complications should arise when the horse is put in the double bridle for the FEI tests. If you need the double bridle as a "break" the training of the horse is wrong. Work your horse mostly in the snaffle but make him familiar with the double bridle.

36

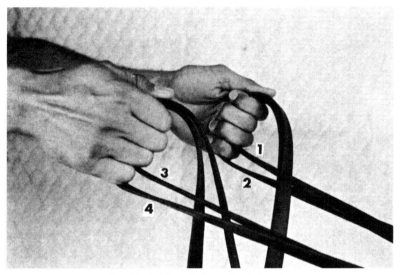

Double Bridle—Reins in Both Hands
1. *Left Curb Rein*   3. *Right Curb Rein*
2. *Left Snaffle Rein*   4. *Right Snaffle Rein*

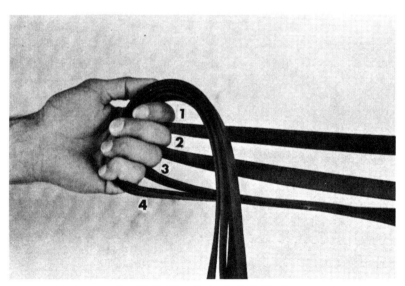

Double Bridle—Reins in Left Hand
1. *Right Snaffle Rein* 3. *Left Curb Rein*
2. *Right Curb Rein*   4. *Left Snaffle Rein*

37

Increasing the Pressure on the Bit
First Action—Close Your Fist

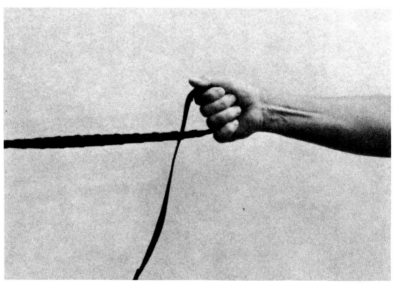

Next Action—If Necessary, Turn Your Hand in the Vertical Line
So Your Little Finger Comes Closer to Your Body

38

When increasing the pressure of the bit, first close your fist (squeeze the reins); then, if necessary, turn your hand in the vertical line so your little finger comes closer to your body. If this is not enough, move the whole system (upper and lower arms and hands) backward. This movement starts at the shoulders. At the walk on contact, for instance, when your hands follow the nodding of the horse's head, the forward movement starts at your shoulders. Do not just use your hands and fingers by bending your wrists.

Don't lock the neck with your reins. *The length of the reins must be adjusted to the movement the horse performs,* f.i. longer reins at extended walk than at collected walk, because of the longer frame of the horse.

The use of the reins, when increasing the pressure on the bit, does not mean a long stubborn pull. It means short repeated actions. As soon as the horse obeys, the hands must relax. *It is the giving, not the pulling, which gets results.*

THE WEIGHT

The rider uses his *weight* to adjust himself to the horse's center of gravity or to change the horse's center of gravity as the horse reacts to the displacement of the rider's weight. Thus the weight can temporarily be moved *slightly* forward or backward or to one side to obtain a desired reaction. For instance, by placing his weight more on the inside* sitting bone, lowering the inside knee and pushing the inside hip slightly forward, the rider, *without changing the position of his seat,* can cause the horse to turn in that direction. This "sitting inward" is often misinterpreted. The rider still sits over the middle of the horse with increased pressure on the inside seatbone. This pressure is obtained by bearing down

---

* Inside is the direction in which the horse is or is supposed to be bent. Generally, but not always, the inside faces the arena. At countercanter or turn on forehand, for instance, the inside faces the wall.

on the heel. The rider should not lean inward or collapse his hip. In such case he slides outward, looses the balance and the ability to push the horse forward.

The rider's hips and shoulders should always remain parallel to those of the horse.

SPURS AND WHIP — THE VOICE

Spurs are not necessary, but are a required part of the equipment at FEI level tests. A horse should be trained to respond to light aids without spurs. However, when spurs are necessary, use blunt ones. Spurs should be used to refine the aids, not to amplify them.

The whip is a good aid to support the leg. On a schooled horse it is used as a reminder. The whip should be fairly stiff and of such length that you can use it behind your lower leg (a short tap) without moving your hand backward or removing it from the rein. Sometimes the whip can be used as a punishment. This must be done in connection with the "crime," otherwise the horse cannot understand why he is punished. By this I mean, the whip must be used when and where the "crime" is committed, never after the fact. The whip should be carried on the side where you need it.

Use your voice as a training aid, much as you would use the whip, as a reward or punishment. Clicking of the tongue is a helpful reminder to the horse. However, use of the voice and tongue must not become a habit of which the rider is unaware. Nor can it become a substitute for the seat and legs.

Remember, you are penalized for using your voice or tongue during a dressage test.

INFLUENCE AND COORDINATION OF THE AIDS

Bending refers to lateral bending. Flexion refers to longitudinal bending, specifically the poll and jaw. A horse is correctly bent when the rider can see the superciliary arch above the eye and the nostril.

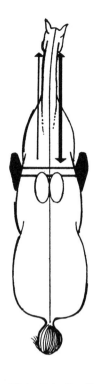 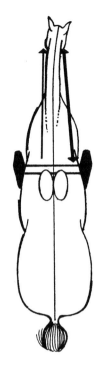 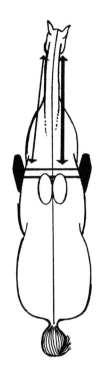

Right Rein Bending—
Left Rein Controlling
the Bend

Right Rein Leading
(Supporting)—Left
Rein Controlling
the Bend

Right Rein Bending—
Left Rein Leading (for
Instance, Young Horse
at Corners)

When both legs squeeze, the horse should go forward. When the pressure of one leg is stronger, he should move sideways. Remember that this influence originates from a firm seat. Both legs cooperate. At lateral work, for instance, when you squeeze with your inside leg, the outside leg should keep contact. The more contact, the more influence. The effect of the squeezing leg stays within the horse.

As illustrated, your hands move toward your body (bending) or toward your hip (leading or supporting). They should never move across the mane. Imagine that there is a wall between your two hands which cannot be climbed or pushed away. The hands, as well as the legs, must cooperate. One rein should not be loose.

41

What you take with one hand must be given by the other. If you bend your horse on a curved line, you keep the outside rein taut to control the bend of the horse. When the hands cooperate, the bit stays in the middle of the horse's mouth. It should never be pulled out of the mouth to one side.

All the aids must be brought into harmonious cooperation.

Let us ride a transition. A smooth transition must start from behind with engagement of the hindquarters. If you go from a halt into walk, from walk to trot, from trot to canter or vice versa, you must use *your seat* and *your legs* in the same way. Sit deeper and firmer (tighten your seat, brace your back) and feel that you grow taller. Your knees and heels are lowered and you grip your horse with your lower legs behind the girth. If you want to go forward or into a faster pace, *relax your hands*. If you want to slow down or ride a halt, *set your hands*.

HALF-HALT

Using the aids in this way within a pace or changing from one pace to another is called a *HALF-HALT*. Half-parade is a more adequate expression, since you should not think of a halt at all.

A half-halt is a barely visible, almost simultaneous, coordinated action of the seat, legs and hands of the rider, the object being to increase the attention and balance of the horse before the execution of several movements, or of transitions to lesser or higher paces. By shifting more weight onto the horse's quarters, the engagement of the hind legs and the balance on the haunches

42

are facilitated. This is essential to achieve lightness of the fore-hand and the horse's balance as a whole. The horse should offer no resistance to the rider's hands.

A *half-halt* is a call for attention to make the horse alert and ready for action. The activity behind is increased. A half-halt performed with a pulling hand and no driving of seat and legs is more damaging than helpful.

The half-halt is an excellent means of developing the horse, as well as the rider's seat and use of the aids.

There are many degrees of half-halts and the requirements should be increased as the training of the horse progresses. A green horse should not be asked for much engagement, and will probably resist the bit in the beginning. Do not hang on stub-bornly. If the half-halt does not work, repeat it. Inhale-exhale, that is the length of a half-halt. After the half-halt resume the rhythm. Never let the horse go faster and run away from your aids.

Prepare for every exercise by using a half-halt. If the horse is sluggish or goes too fast, use repeated half-halts. Gradually, when the horse is supple and obedient, the half-halts are refined and almost invisible. On a well schooled horse the half-halt con-sists of a firmer seat and a slight squeeze of the reins. Invisible, but the horse feels it and understands the signal which says: "be alert, listen to me." Throughout all training, use half-halts frequently.

A half-halt forces the rider to sit correctly and coordinate his aids. A well executed half-halt proves that the horse and the rider are correctly trained.

UNILATERAL AIDS

Another fundamental principle is the coordination of the *leg and the rein on the same side* known as *the unilateral aids*. The rein controls the haunches and supports the leg on the same side. If the rein is used toward the rider's hip, the horse will swing his haunches. This knowledge is used when training a horse to obey

43

the leg. The more obedient the horse becomes to the leg, the less the rein is needed. However, even a well schooled horse needs a little check on the rein as a reminder. The importance of the unilateral aids will be pointed out many times in this manual. The unilateral aids are, for instance, used for riding through corners, for all lateral work, for turns on the forehand and half-turns on the haunches. Only when the horse is obedient to the unilateral aids is it time to start with the diagonal aids.

RESUMÉ OF COORDINATION OF AIDS

In this manual, seat and legs are called pushing aids and the hands are stopping aids. *The pushing aids must dominate.* Ride your horse forward with your seat and legs—guide him and give him signals with your reins. The reins are there so the rider can tell him *not* to lean on the bit.

The "feel" of the rider is a divine gift. It means that the rider feels when the rhythm is right, when the horse swings his back and when the contact is ideal. It also means that the rider can time the aids and bring them into harmonious coordination and use them in proportion to the desired effect. This feel can be developed if the rider always tries to find out how the horse reacts to his aids. When the horse performs well, then your aids are correct. However, if the training goes poorly, you should first ask yourself: what am I doing wrong? It is seldom the horse which is to blame when the training does not go well.

The rider must be consistent and give clear signals to avoid misunderstandings.

Chapter III

LONGEING AND MOUNTING THE GREEN HORSE

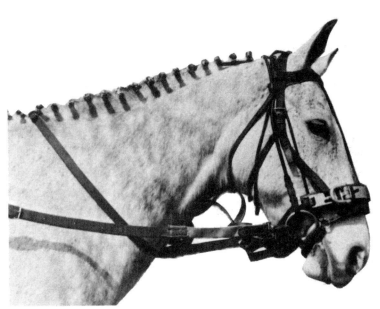

Prepared for Longeing
Snaffle, longeing cavesson and side reins

The purpose of longeing the green horse is to make him familiar with the bit, to teach him obedience to the pushing and stopping aids, and to improve his balance in order to make it easier for him to carry the rider's weight. Therefore, a cavesson should be used. The cavesson represents the stopping aids (the reins) and the longeing whip is the pushing aid (the legs). The trainer's voice can support both pushing and stopping aids.

The cavesson must be carefully fitted and the throatlash tightened so the horse's eye cannot be injured.

Longeing in a halter has no schooling purpose, as the trainer has no control of the horse. Longeing with the line attached to the bit affects the horse's mouth when the trainer wants to stop the horse, to slow down the speed or to punish him and can easily ruin the horse's mouth. Longeing, when done correctly, is a very good means of training the horse. Performed by a dilettante, it can be more detrimental than a razor in the hands of a monkey.

To begin with, only the cavesson should be used. After a few days the horse should be tacked with a snaffle and a saddle without stirrups. The girth should not be too tight, but tight enough so that the saddle cannot slip.

In the beginning, side reins should be used,* loosely attached to a surcingle or to the girth, with both reins the same length. As the work progresses they should be shortened so the horse can take a light contact. The horse, however, should always be able to carry his nose in front of the vertical.

At the walk, the side reins should often be detached so as to permit the horse to use his neck and stretch it forward. Short side reins restrict the length of the strides and can damage a good natural walk.

Boots should be used on all four legs to prevent the horse from hitting himself.

An assistant should be used during the first lessons. Since the whip represents the most important aids (the pushing), the trainer should handle the whip and the assistant the longeing line. Let us suppose that the horse is working on the right rein. The trainer leads the horse on the circle with his left hand, keeping the whip (the lash pointing backward) in his right. The voice must be used, supporting the pushing or stopping aids, rewarding or scolding the horse.

When the horse walks on, the trainer moves away from him toward the center of the circle and takes the whip in his left hand. The whip points toward the girth or the hindquarters to urge the horse forward. If the horse tries to move inward, the

---

*Note: when longeing a trained horse, side reins are not necessary.

Longeing With an Assistant
The Horse "On the Bit" Keeps the Line Taut

whip is pointed toward his head. The assistant regulates the rhythm by short actions on the line. There must be good cooperation between the trainer and the assistant (two souls and one thought). When the horse moves quietly, the trainer takes over the line and handles both the whip and the line. The assistant should remain behind him, keeping the end of the line, so that the trainer can hand over the line and walk up to the horse if he stops or turns inward and can lead him out again on the circle. The trainer must be patient and, especially at transitions, quietly try, again and again, until the horse obeys.

To begin with, the work should be done at walk and trot. When the trot is stabilized, it is time to longe at the canter. At the outset it is advisable to diminish the circle a little and, when the horse increases the circle again, urge him into canter. Thus he will be a little more alert and engaged.

47

Longeing Without an Assistant
The Horse Remains "On the Bit"

The horse should keep the longeing line stretched, maintaining the same light contact as he later on will be asked to do on the rein. At halts, the horse should stop on the track of the circle and stand still on contact. When the trainer wants to change the rein or finish the lesson, the horse must first stand still. The trainer should then walk up to the horse. If the horse is taught to come to the trainer, he develops the habit of diminishing the circle and moving at halts.

When the horse understands the aids and moves quietly, the rider can mount. This should be done before the horse becomes too strong and conscious of his power. The first time there should be one assistant on each side of the horse, putting more and more weight (pull) on the leathers to make the horse familiar with the weight. Next time, the rider is lifted up in the saddle and remains for a while, with both legs on the same side. This procedure is repeated until the horse stands quietly. Then, the rider swings his right leg over the back of the horse and sinks quietly into the

48

saddle. The trainer handles the cavesson while standing at the horse's head. The rider should not use the reins or squeeze with his lower legs. Then the horse is quietly led forward. Once in the saddle, the rider must stay on, even if the horse tries to get rid. of him. A stirrup leather fastened around the neck of the horse or a grip of the mane can be helpful to the rider's security.

Now the horse is worked in the same way as without a rider. When the horse is confident, the rider takes a light contact on the reins (without pulling) and starts to use his legs to urge the horse forward. The trainer, with whip, cavesson and voice, supports him. Finally the cavesson can be removed and the rider is on his own. The serious training of the horse can now begin.

Chapter IV

TRAINING OF THE YOUNG OR UNTRAINED HORSE

GENERAL PRINCIPLES

The main purpose is to maintain and stabilize his desire to go forward and gradually develop his obedience to the aids.

Obedience to the aids is a condition for suppleness. Without suppleness it is impossible to bend, flex or engage the horse in the correct way. And, paradoxically, if you cannot bend your horse, you cannot make him straight. So it all starts with obedience to the aids.

To create this obedience, the following exercises can be used:

Riding straight forward

Turns through the corner

Turns across the diagonal, down the center line and across the arena

Circles

Half-circles and half-circles in reverse

Serpentine along the long side and across the center line

Change of circles

Change of rein through the circle

Figure of eight

Decreasing and increasing the circle

Leg yielding

Turn on the forehand

To start with, the horse should be worked at walk and trot. When the trot is stabilized in a reasonable way, the work at canter can begin.

50

Ride the walk as a free walk on long reins. Gradually pick up a very light contact, only the weight of the reins. Do not push him together, only urge him forward with your legs and the whip. The trot should be a lively working trot without hurry. It is easier for a young horse to carry himself in a lively rhythm. Use soft short pulls on the inside rein to guide him. Perform the transitions very progressively. At halts let him *stand still*, and do not worry much about the position of his legs. A correct halt will be required later on. Post at the trot, but drive the horse forward when posting. Later on, alternate between posting and sitting trot. Posting trot is ridden on the outside diagonal, which means that you sit when the outside foreleg is on the ground. The support in the stirrups should be taken in the *vertical line*, not forward or outward. Do not work with your body too much. Let the horse lift you up while you keep your hands steady.

The horse should seek the contact forward by lowering and lengthening the neck. The contact should never be obtained by moving the hands backward. The hands must be quiet and passive. The correct contact cannot be established until the horse obeys the pushing aids. He must be worked from the rear to the front, with the neck remaining long. If he plays with the bit or drops it, urge him forward with legs and whip. The rhythm is of primary importance. The rider must try to maintain a steady rhythm and the same length of the strides. Every horse has a rhythm in which he is happy. The differences can be very small. The trot, for instance, can be slightly hurried or a little too slow. If you are not sure, ask somebody with more experience and "eye" and feel for the rhythm to help you on the ground and tell you when the horse is in harmony. Keeping a steady rhythm is an excellent way to discipline a horse. When the rhythm is stabilized, then and only then, can you start to increase and decrease the tempo.

Do not confine your work to the enclosed arena. It can make the horse bored. Vary the training and the surroundings to maintain the willingness forward.

51

RIDING STRAIGHT FORWARD

No horse is absolutely straight. Every horse has a hollow and a stiff side. The right side is generally the hollow one, which means that he is not accepting the bit on the right side, saves his right hind and travels with the hind legs to the right of the track of the front legs. He is not on a single track. How to straighten a horse will be dealt with later on. To begin with, try to keep him as straight as possible and urge him forward.

TURN THROUGH THE CORNER

In the beginning, make the corners round and shallow, then gradually narrow them. The inside rein leads the horse into the

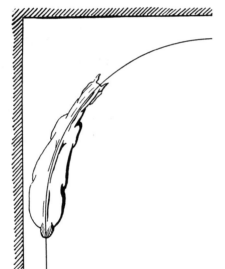

turn and the inside leg pushes him outward. If necessary, the outside rein leads him out into the corner without losing the proper bend.

The turn, however, should be performed mainly by the inside leg in coordination with the inside rein. This is the first exercise to develop obedience to the unilateral aids. Both legs push the horse forward. At the same time, in cooperation with the reins, they adjust the horse to the curved line so that the hind legs move in the same

tracks as the front legs. The inside leg is kept on the girth and the outside behind the girth to prevent the horse from swinging the haunches out. The outside rein controls the bend. Don't overbend the horse. Overbending causes the horse to lose his balance, swing outward, and fall onto the outside shoulder. This is a common mistake, because a horse will often bend his neck too much when asked to bend his whole body. Make sure that

52

his neck is not bent more than his body. The rider sits inward by bearing down on the inside heel, as explained under Weight Influence, chapter II. The outside shoulder is moved slightly forward, so that the rider's shoulders remain parallel to the horse's shoulders.

Most horses will push in (cut the corner). This is prevented by a leading outside rein and a squeezing inside leg, if necessary supported by the inside rein. After the corner the horse must be straightened by the outside rein and pushed forward in the new direction. When changing direction at right angles, for instance, when riding through corners or turning across the arena, the radius should not be larger than the maximum circle requirements in the particular test. At collected paces, however, the horse should describe one quarter of a circle of approximately 6 meters diameter and at medium and extended paces one quarter of a circle of approximately 10 meters diameter.

If you try to ride the corners accurately, you will find that this simple exercise gives an amazingly good result.

Some higher level tests include medium or extended paces through the corners. Remember that you are permitted to cut the corners a little, which makes it easier to maintain the rhythm and the balance.

TURN ACROSS THE DIAGONAL, DOWN THE CENTER LINE AND ACROSS THE ARENA

These are performed in the same way as turning through the corners. It is important to use the outside aids to prevent the horse from swinging outward and to straighten him after the turn.

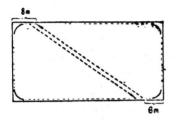

CHANGE OF REIN ACROSS THE DIAGONAL

At meeting (pass left hand to left hand) you arrive at the opposite long side 8 meters from the corner, otherwise 6 meters.

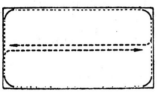

DOWN THE CENTER LINE

If several riders are performing this movement at the same time from both short sides, the turn should be done 1 meter in front of the middle of the short side (A and C).

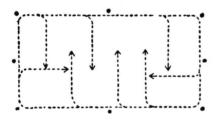

TURNS ACROSS THE ARENA

Prepare for the turn with a half-halt. Use the outside aids to prevent the horse from overbending and drifting outward.

CIRCLES

The diameter of a circle is larger than 6 meters. If the diameter is 6 meters or smaller the figure is called a volte. It must be finished where it was started. The horse should adjust the bend of his body to the size of the circle and move on a single track. A steady rhythm and the same length of the strides should be maintained.

A circle is round, not oval or like a loop. It

As a preparation for the circle, make him ready for action by riding a half-halt and, while maintaining the rhythm, sit inward (without leaning) and lead the horse into the circle with the inside rein. The inside rein and the inside leg on the girth bend him slightly (you should see the arch above the inside eye and the nostril). Keep the outside rein taut to control (limit) the bend. Your outside leg behind the girth controls the haunches. Haunches swinging in means not enough use of the inside leg and too much use of the outside leg. The lower legs, as usual, must be flexible. For instance, if the horse swings the haunches in, your inside leg should be used behind the girth. If he leans on the outside shoulder, use the outside leg on the girth.

Again, be careful not to overbend the horse. Do not pull the horse around the circle by hanging on your inside rein. Control the bend with the outside rein. The use of the outside rein improves the carriage and the rhythm. Sometimes during schooling, bend the horse *outward* for a couple of strides; this is a good way to control the outside shoulder.

If the horse tends to diminish the size of the circle, move him out again by the unilateral aids (the inside leg and rein). The outside rein, as discussed previously, leads him out while maintaining the proper bend of the circle. In other words, push the inside aids toward the outside aids.

55

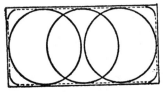

Big Circles in the Arena

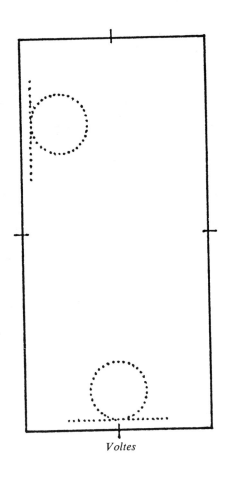

Voltes

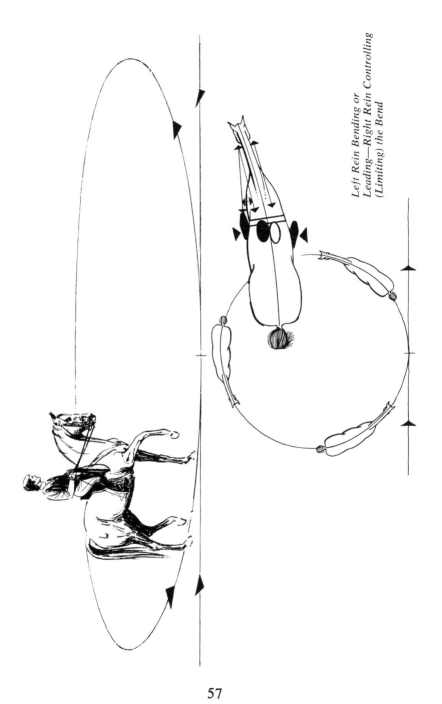

*Left Rein Bending or
Leading—Right Rein Controlling
(Limiting) the Bend*

57

HALF-CIRCLES AND HALF-CIRCLES IN REVERSE

These figures are ridden in the same way as the circles. If the diameter is 6 meters or smaller, the figure is called half-volte. After the half-circle, the horse is returned to the track on a straight line, which is an oblique angle to the track. It is useful to combine these two exercises. Ride a half-circle immediately followed by a half-circle in reverse.

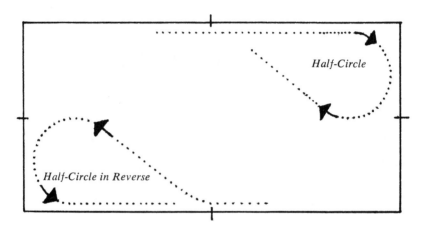

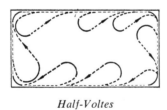

Half-Voltes

SERPENTINE ALONG THE LONG SIDE

In the beginning, this should be performed with one shallow loop. Leave the long side, go to the quarter line and return to the long side. When coming back to the long side, turn your horse accurately through the corner.

58

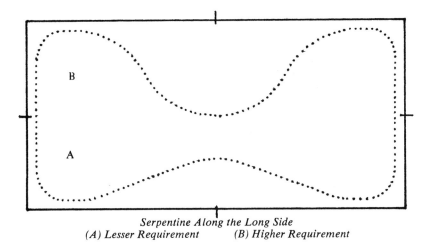

Serpentine Along the Long Side
(A) Lesser Requirement   (B) Higher Requirement

SERPENTINE ACROSS THE CENTER LINE

To begin with, this should be ridden with a few (2-3) big flat loops. Cross the center line at about right angles and make the horse straight for a horse length. Prepare for the change of direction by a half-halt.

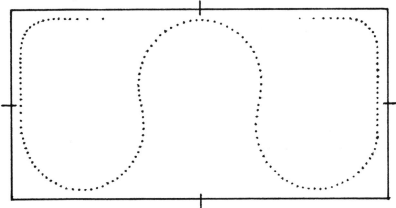

Serpentine Across the Center Line

The number of loops is prescribed in the test. The first loop is started by moving gradually away from the middle of the short side of the arena, and the last loop is finished by moving gradually toward the middle of the opposite short side. Starting and finishing by riding into the corners is incorrect. Examples of serpentines with four and six loops see Appendix.

59

If the exercises described above are performed at a steady rising trot and the rider tries to bend the horse correctly at the corners and on curved lines, every horse will sooner or later settle down, find his harmony and accept the bit.

✳ ✳ ✳

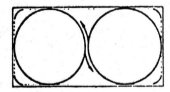
THE CHANGE OF CIRCLES
Cross the center line at a right angle. Perform a half-halt and change the bend. Bear down on the inside heel.

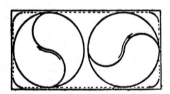
THE CHANGE OF REIN THROUGH THE CIRCLE
Perform a half-halt and change the bend at the center of the circle. Put more weight on the inside seatbone. Don't let the horse drift out on the half-circles.

THE FIGURE OF EIGHT
The figure consists of exact voltes or circles of equal size as prescribed in the test. Make your horse straight an instant before changing direction at the center of the figure.

The figure of eight is often ridden with the center at X either after a turn down the center line or a turn from the middle of the long side.

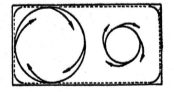
DECREASING AND INCREASING THE CIRCLE
Diminish the circle gradually by spiralling inward. Maintain the bend and the rhythm. It is more difficult to maintain the rhythm on a smaller circle. Increase the circle by spiralling out of it. Lead with the outer rein without bending outward. This exercise will be used later on in connection with lateral work.

60

Riding on curved lines with frequent changes of rein will develop the horse's balance, suppleness and obedience. Correct bending is essential. It makes him obedient, stretches his muscles on the outside and relaxes those on the inside.

The previous exercises, corners, circles, serpentines and such, can be seen as simply a variety of ways to present to the horse the curved lines and changes in his bending needed to achieve these goals. Riding curved lines in a number of ways maintains the horse's attention and lessens the chance of disobedience from boredom.

LEG YIELDING

Leg yielding, like the turn on the forehand, is a basic exercise. It is often advisable to start leg yielding before the turn on the forehand, because it is easier to influence a horse in motion. On the other hand, it is easier to control the horse on the spot (less pulling).

The purpose of leg yielding is:

1. to make the horse obedient to the unilateral aids (legs and hands on the same side), thus suppling him and preparing him for the shoulder-in, the half-pass, travers (haunches-in) and renvers (haunches-out).

   Leg yielding is a means to make the horse obedient, not an end in itself.

2. to teach the rider to use the aids.

As opposed to the other lateral movements, leg yielding can be executed at a training level where the horse is not yet ready for collected movements. The horse is slightly bent at the poll, so that the rider is just able to see the eyebrow and the nostril on the inside, looking away from the direction in which he is moving and straight along the spine.

61

Leg yielding can be ridden (see pictures):

1. away from the long side
2. away from the long side and back to the long side
3. along the long side
4. across the diagonal
5. on circles

KAY MEREDITH
Leg Yielding Across the Diagonal—The Horse Is Moving to the Left,
Bent Slightly to the Right

You can give your horse his first lesson in leg yielding while dismounted. For instance, hold him with the left rein in your left hand, close to the bit. Touch him with the whip behind the girth. When he moves the haunches, relax your left hand so he can move one or two steps diagonally forward. The idea is to teach him to yield to the whip and not to the rein. The rein supports the whip when necessary. Change sides and repeat the exercise in the other direction.

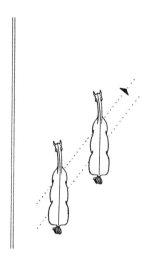

Leg Yielding Away from the Long Side

The easiest way to teach a horse leg yielding while mounted, is to move him away from the long side of the wall (see picture). The willingness to move forward can always be controlled by going more freely straight forward whenever you want to.

If you have the chance to ride on a road with good footing (a dirt road or a sandy road), you can teach your horse leg yielding by moving him from one side of the road to the other.

Let us imagine that you are now on the right rein at medium walk. After the corner, make a soft half-halt and bend the horse slightly to the left at the poll. You should see the arch

63

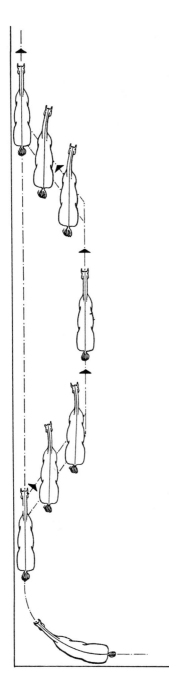

above the left eye and the left nostril. Both legs maintain the impulsion. Increase the pressure of your left leg behind the girth and push him sideways. The position of the left leg must be *flexible*. Move it forward to the girth if the forehand resists and you want more effect on the forehand. The left leg, if necessary, is supported by the left rein (used toward the body or toward the hip, but never across the mane). The right time to squeeze the left leg is when the left hind leaves the ground.

If the horse does not obey your leg, give him a short, sharp kick and support the leg with the whip. Remember that you must teach him obedience to the leg. You can also support the leg with the rein by moving it toward the hip in order to force him to swing (move) the haunches. This should be done temporarily, and the horse must be straightened in the next stride.

The right rein leads the horse away from the long side (he is still slightly bent to the left). The right leg is used on the girth to maintain impulsion, keep him straight and prevent him from overbending. Used in combination with the right rein, this also keeps him from escaping the pressure of the left leg and

Leg Yielding Away from the
Long Side and Back to the Long Side

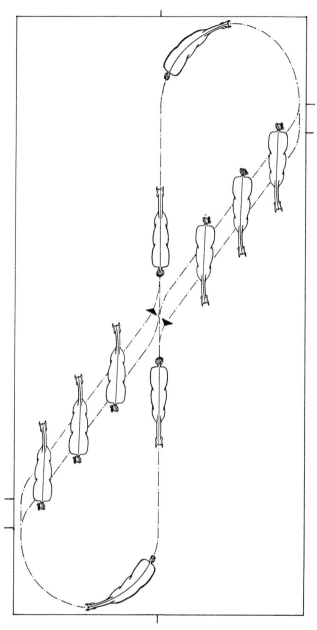

Leg Yielding Across Half a Diagonal and
Straight Forward on Center Line

65

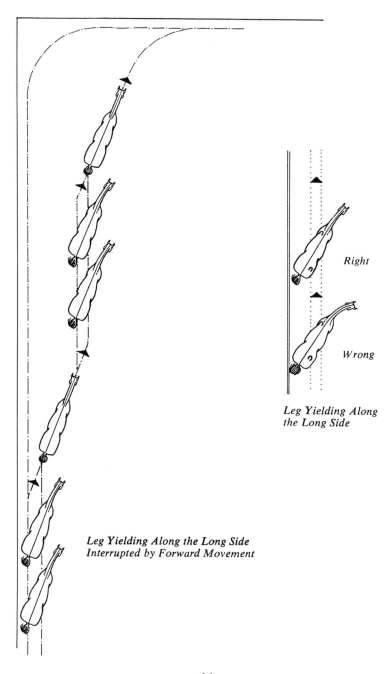

Right

Wrong

Leg Yielding Along the Long Side

Leg Yielding Along the Long Side
Interrupted by Forward Movement

from moving crosswise too much. The outside leg must be *flexible* too. If the haunches are leading, use your outside leg behind the girth. It is important to keep the right leg close to the horse.

When you want him to go straight forward, reduce the pressure of the left leg and increase the pressure of the right leg and push him forward with both legs.

It is important to sit over the middle of the horse. Do not collapse your inside hip, thus sliding out of the saddle. Ask for only a few strides in the beginning. Go forward and then resume the exercise. *Do not lose the willingness to go forward by executing this exercise for a long period of time.*

The horse should be almost parallel to the long side. The shoulders, however, should lead slightly. It is a serious fault to overbend the horse. Leg yielding should be started and taught at the walk. Later on it should preferably be ridden at the trot, as it is easier at the trot to maintain the willingness forward and create impulsion. Maintaining a steady rhythm is important.

When leg yielding along the long side (see picture), the forehand moves inside the track at an angle of about 35°. Try to keep the rhythm and sometimes ride straight forward out of the leg yielding diagonally across the arena or go forward along the track.

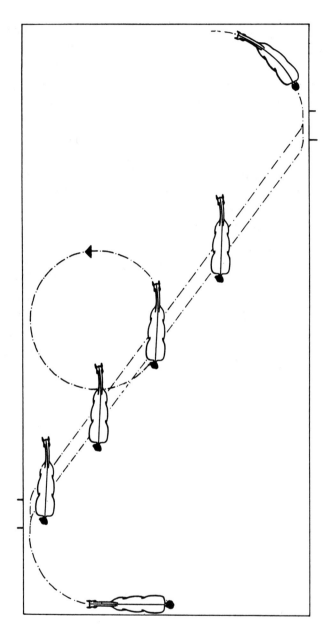

Leg Yielding Across the Diagonal
Interrupted by a Circle

68

When riding leg yielding on a circle, spiral in to a smaller circle as you do when you diminish the circle, and then push the horse back out to the larger circle in leg yielding. This is a very good exercise to supple the horse and to make him accept the bit. The horse should be adjusted to the curvature of the circle. Again, be sure not to overbend the horse and let the haunches swing outward.

Test his obedience by riding leg yielding across the whole diagonal. And sometimes, when you execute this exercise, ride a circle at X, then resume the leg yielding.

The obedience and suppleness is gradually developed until the horse obeys light, invisible aids and moves in a supple, balanced way, either away from the long side or along the long side. The horse should be trained at leg yielding until he is absolutely obedient to the unilateral aids and ready for at least modestly collected paces. When he fullfills these requirements, it is time to introduce the shoulder-in and the half-pass.

Shoulder-in is developed from leg yielding along the long side by engaging him more and by gradually bending him uniformly along the spine from the tail to the poll.

The half-pass is developed from leg yielding away from the long side, and then gradually engaging him more and bending him into the direction in which he is moving. If you have been able to ride him straight at leg yielding and he is obedient also to your outside leg, it is obvious that it will now be easy to bend him into the direction he is moving.

THE TURN ON THE FOREHAND

The turn on the forehand is a basic exercise. In the same way as you did at leg yielding, you can give your horse the first lesson while dismounted. The aids for the turn are the same as for leg yielding. The difference is that, instead of going forward, you move him around the inside front leg. Practice leg yielding before you start the turn on the forehand.

The purpose of the turn is to supple the horse and to teach him obedience to the aids. The turn is fairly easy to perform,

69

KAY MEREDITH
*Turn on the Forehand—The Inside Left Hind Leg Strikes the Ground
in Front of the Right Hind Leg*

70

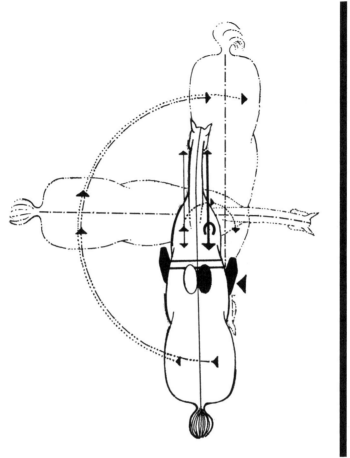

The Turn on the Forehand

but the rider must execute it under full control of himself and the horse.

Before you turn, ride one stride inside the track (the wall) to give clearance to the horse's head. Ride the halt and let the horse stand still before you turn. The inside fore-foot, as explained in footnote, page 39, is the pivot, stepping all the time, not stuck to the ground or twisting. The outside fore-foot steps forward and around the inside forefoot, and the hind feet move on a curved line, the inside hind foot striking the ground in front of the outside. The horse is slightly bent to the inside.

You are now on the left rein (see drawing). You move him with the unilateral aids. After the halt, bend him *slightly* (you should see the arch above the eye, not more) by closing the right fist. More weight on the right seatbone. Squeeze with your right leg behind the girth, (not on the rib cage) and move him, step by step. If the horse wants to go backward, urge him forward with both legs. If he wants to go forward, tighten your reins. Your left leg on the girth controls the speed (he must move step by step without rushing) and moves the left fore-foot forward. If he swings the haunches too fast, use your left leg behind the girth. The left rein controls the bend. When you have completed the turn, straighten your horse and walk on.

Use your legs, do not turn him with the reins. Do not let him move backward. If he does, stop the exercise, urge him forward, straighten him and try again. Do not overbend him (too much inside rein, not enough outside leg on the girth). Ride step by step. Do not twist your upper body to give the inside leg more strength.

It is often helpful to use the whip behind your inside leg. The aim, however, is to make the horse obedient to a slight squeeze— a whisper.

THE CANTER

The right lead on the right rein or the left lead on the left rein is called the true canter. The left lead on the right rein or vice versa is called the counter-canter. If the horse picks up the left lead on the right rein or vice versa, against the rider's will, it is called the false canter.

At the departure, the horse must think forward. Call him to attention by a half-halt. Sit inward, lower your inside knee. Squeeze the inside rein a little more than the outside. Do not

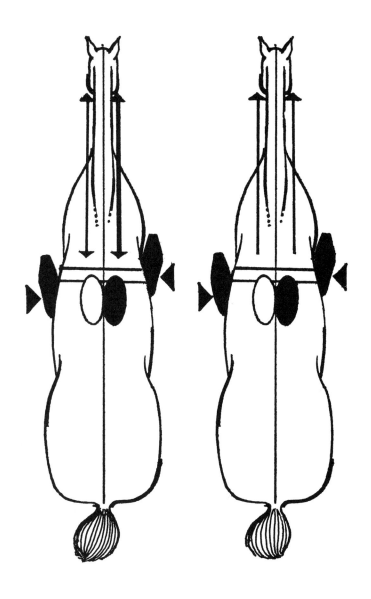

The Canter Departure Right Lead
Phase 1. The Aids   *Phase 2. Relaxation of the Hands*

73

bend the horse outward. Keep your inside leg at the girth and the outside leg behind the girth and urge him into canter by squeezing with *both* legs. Do not forget to squeeze with your outside leg. He starts the canter with his outside hind leg. If he gets used to the signal with the outside leg, it will be easy, later on, to teach him flying changes. As soon as he strikes off, relax your inside hand so he can reach forward with his leading leg.

The correct time to give the aids, when you depart from the trot, is when the inside front leg touches the ground. From the walk it is when the outside front leg touches the ground.

After the departure, your outside leg must be flexible. Move it forward to the girth to control the outside shoulder, or if you feel that he is cantering with the haunches inside the track.

At the beginning, ride the transition into canter from the trot. When he strikes off quietly and easily from the trot, depart from the walk. Gradually reduce the number of intermediate strides at the trot until he strikes off directly from the walk. The departure from the walk is a good exercise because the horse must use his haunches more to lift himself up in the air.

Common faults at the departure are when the rider looks down to the inside shoulder, collapses the inside hip and leans forward and inward, causing a wrong influence of the weight. The rider often pulls the inside rein, preventing the horse from moving his inside shoulder and hind leg forward. The rider's outside leg may lose its contact, move too much backward and cause a departure on two tracks.

A good way to teach the horse to depart from trot into canter is as follows. Ride the rising trot at a steady rhythm, change the rein across the diagonal and strike off just before the corner. Do not let him rush. Prepare for the transition by a half-halt and try to "float" into the canter without an explosion. If he rushes, use repeated half-halts and resume the steady trot. Reverse and ride the diagonal again. If he picks up the correct canter, take him once around the arena (make the corners round), break to the trot, change the rein across the diagonal, pick up the other lead, and so on.

74

Prepare for the transition from canter to trot by soft half-halts. Break mainly with your inside aids (unilateral) which give a suppler transition. Use short elastic pulls on the inside rein. Keep your outside rein steady. Move your inside leg slightly backward. As soon as the horse breaks, relax your hands and resume the trot. If he rushes, repeat the half-halt.

Restore the relaxed trot before you ride a diagonal. Even if your horse is a little explosive in the beginning, he will soon settle down.

If he picks up the wrong lead, break immediately to the trot and try again.

At the canter you should follow the movement of the horse in a relaxed way with your seat moving from back to front. If your knee and ankle are stiff, you will bounce up and down in the saddle, making it difficult for the horse to move smoothly. Imagine that you are running with a knapsack badly attached to your back. You will be very irritated as it moves around, bounces and interferes with your motion. A horse will react in the same way to a rider who is loose in the saddle.

When the horse understands the aids, practice the transitions on the big circle, mainly from the walk. To begin with, diminish the circle a little, increase it at leg yielding, thus pushing the inside hind leg under the body of the horse and, upon return to the track of the big circle, go directly into the canter. On the circle the horse should adjust his body to the curved line. Keep him slightly bent with your inside leg on the girth and your inside rein. Prevent the haunches from swinging out with your outside leg. Regulate the speed with repeated elastic pulls on the outside rein. Restore the supple, harmonious medium walk before you strike off again. He should maintain the same frame and the same contact at the departure, and not throw his head up. First control his obedience by several half-halts at the canter, and, when you feel that they go through the body to the haunches, use the opportunity and make the transition.

Sometimes go from the circle around the arena. Maintain the rhythm, do not go faster or increase the number of strides.

Keep him straight along the straight line. If he canters with the hind feet inside the track, use more inside leg and rein and use the outside leg on the girth, controlling the outside shoulder. In the beginning, it is better if he looks a little inward and is not completely straight at the neck, rather than to canter on two tracks (or with the haunches in). Think a little of the shoulder-in.

If the horse is crooked, you lose valuable points in a competition. It is a common fault to permit the horse to move the haunches inward at the departure and at the transition back to the prescribed pace, f.i. from medium canter to collected canter.

You can now also change the rein across the diagonal and change the lead through the trot or through the walk. Between the break and the departure, you must restore a good trot or walk.

Later on, you can ride the simple change of lead, which means that you walk two or three well defined steps before cantering on with the other leg leading.

THE COUNTER-CANTER

When the horse is in balance in the true canter, and is obedient to the aids for the departure, it is time to ride the counter-canter. Counter-canter is a movement where the rider, for instance, on a circle to the left, deliberately makes his horse canter on the right canter lead (with the off-fore leading). The counter-canter is a supling movement. The horse maintains his natural flexion at the poll to the outside of the circle. In other words, he is bent to the side of the leading leg. His conformation does not permit his spine to be bent to the line of the circle. The rider, avoiding any contortion causing contraction and disorder, should specially endeavor to limit the deviation of the quarters to the outside of the circle and restrict his demands according to the degree of suppleness of the horse.

Counter-canter is an excellent schooling exercise. It develops the smoothness, balance and reaction to the aids, and is a good exercise for the rider to coordinate the aids. It is a way to make the horse straight (see Chapter V).

76

The counter-canter is a question of balance. If the horse looses his balance, he will break the canter or go faster. When he goes faster, he comes on his forehand and is inclined to change the lead. The advice is: ride counter-canter as you would ride the true canter by maintaining the *same* rhythm, the *same* bend, the *same* seat and use the *same* aids. If you change your seat, you will disturb the balance. Counter-canter is no problem. The rider creates the problems because he thinks it is difficult. He becomes too ambitious and starts moving around in the saddle. Do not make a great thing of it.

The easiest way to teach the horse the counter-canter is to pick up the lead at the beginning of a long side or to ride a half-circle, retaining the lead upon the return to the long side. You start at the beginning of the long side and, when riding a half-circle, return to the long side as soon as possible to make the exercise easier. You will have more room in front of you before the corner.

Let us imagine that you are on the left rein. Start at the trot. Ride through the corner, perform the half-halt, move the horse away from the long side a couple of strides, bend him slightly to the right, move him back to the long side and depart at the canter. If you do not get the right lead before the middle of the long side, trot on and start again at the next long side. Gradually you learn to depart at the canter on a straight line without moving him away from the track.

To begin with you may either start at the long side, as just described, or ride a half-circle and break to the trot before the corner. If the horse is in good balance, maintain the canter through two corners. Make them round and shallow. Keep a steady outside (left) rein to control the left shoulder, preventing him from changing the lead, and a steady left leg to maintain the canter.

If the horse breaks from the counter-canter, do not push immediately (a very human reaction). If you do, he will probably pick up the left lead and you thus teach him the wrong thing. Instead, restore a good trot, make him alert and start again.

When the horse strikes off from the trot without effort, you

77

may then depart at the canter from the walk and maintain the counter-canter all the way around the arena. Ride several changes of rein across the diagonal or perform a big figure of eight without changing the lead.

COMMON FAULTS AT THE COUNTER-CANTER

The horse may go faster, with a tendency to rush. The weight is too much on the forehand. The horse leans heavily on the bit because the rider does not dare to use his legs and hands to get the horse in proper balance, being afraid the horse will misinterpret his aids as an invitation to a change of leg. The result is often inactive, dragging quarters, sometimes leading to an irregular four beat canter.

The horse may be bent too much to the leading leg, often in combination with too much deviation of the quarters to the same side.

The horse may not be sufficiently bent, or bent to the wrong side.

The horse may not be straight along straight lines; the haunches may swing out on curved lines.

Chapter V

TO MAKE THE HORSE STRAIGHT

A primary condition for engagement (collection) of the horse is straightness. First straightness, then collection. It is therefore necessary to deal with straightness before proceeding to collection.

No horse is absolutely straight. He is crooked when his forehand and haunches move on different tracks against the rider's will. Such a horse has a stiff (convex) side and a hollow (concave) side. If he, for instance, is stiff to the left, he pushes his left shoulder out, leans more heavily on the left rein, bends too much to the right and carries the haunches to the right. He steps shorter on the hollow, right side, to avoid bending the joints (the stifle, the hock and the fetlock) of his right hind leg and avoids moving it straight forward under the body. The effect of the reins does not go through to the haunches. Consequently the horse must be straightened before he can be engaged.

Crooked Horse

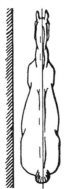

Straight Horse

79

When straightening a horse the idea is to loosen and lighten the contact on the stiff side and encourage him to seek more contact on the hollow side.

Let us suppose that the horse is stiff to the left. Ride him at a working trot on the right rein along straight lines to start with. Both legs drive him forward but the *right (or inside) leg behind the girth* should be used with more strength to urge him to use his right hind leg, to accept the bit, and to prevent him from carrying his right hind leg more to the right. Use your *left (or outside) leg on the girth* to control the left shoulder and to bring it over to the right.

Keep your right hand *quiet* and offer him the contact. Use short, soft pulls on the left rein to loosen up the resistance and prevent him from bending too much to the inside. No long, stubborn pulls, as this only makes the problem worse. The crookedness at the canter should be eliminated in the same way. The inside leg is used behind the girth to prevent the haunches from falling in.

If this method does not work, turn him repeatedly to the left (the stiff) side. As the horse's weight tends outward at the turn, he is mechanically inclined to lean more on the outside (right) rein. Be attentive to maintain this contact.

Now that you have established contact on the right rein, use the right rein to move the right hind leg under the body. If this works, the horse is straight.

You can also use the serpentine along the long side, the purpose being to move the shoulders away from the long side. Maintain the above mentioned position of your legs.

Leg yielding away from your right leg (right leg behind the girth, left on the girth) is another useful exercise.

The left shoulder-in can loosen up the tension in his neck and make him accept the right rein better.

The counter-canter, too, is a useful exercise. If the right hind leg is lazy, ride right lead counter-canter.

All of the above exercises should simply be reversed for a horse who is stiff to the right and hollow to the left.

Chapter VI

THE DEVELOPMENT OF THE HORSE

GENERAL PRINCIPLES

You have now laid a good foundation for continued collected work. The horse accepts the bit, he is supple, straight and his three paces are good or better.

Here are some principles which will help you to get a better and quicker result. You have, of course, observed some of them during the basic training of your horse.

Ride and Then Relax

There is no other alternative. Nothing in between. It is better to ride with concentration for 10 minutes than to move around for 30 minutes without purpose. When relaxing, give yourself and your horse a rest, walk on long reins or dismount. Do not go on nagging.

Maintain the harmonious rhythm and the pure paces

Maintain energy in the paces, but do not hurry. There must be relaxation without slackness. Do not ignore the work at the walk. It is important and gives result.

Ride correct paces

Observe the differences between the paces and emphasize them. You should always decide and know what pace you are riding. It is a good way to school yourself and your horse and develop your feel. There must, for instance, be a clear difference between the working, the medium and the extended trot.

Supple your horse before the commencement of every exercise

If the horse resists, take him on the circle, supple him, establish rhythm and harmony and start again. It is a waste of time to try to perform movements on a resisting horse. The quickest way to teach him is always to teach him the right thing. Be meticulous and patient and he will soon understand that he cannot escape.

Use half-halts frequently

They will be very useful now, as you begin to transfer more weight from the forehand to the haunches. And again, the half-halt is a call to attention when the horse is lazy or resistant. Remember that the purpose is to increase activity behind. A half-halt performed only by the pulling hands without the driving seat and the active legs is useless.

Ride with your legs, guide with your hands

Finish every lesson with an exercise which the horse can easily perform and part as friends

Do not finish with a failure. Expecting too much can never hasten development.

COLLECTION

Now that your horse has gained muscular strength, is supple and straight, you can start to ask for slight collection at the trot and canter. Wait a little before asking for collection at the walk.

There are many degrees of collection—from being on the forehand to the perfection of balance. The degree of collection must be adapted to the phase of training and to the conformation of the horse. Collection must be built up and come as a result of your work. It is detrimental to force the horse into collection.

The aim of collection is:

1. to further develop and improve the balance and equilibrium of the horse, which has been more or less displaced by the additional weight of the rider;

2. to develop and increase the horse's ability to lower and engage his quarters for the benefit of the lightness and mobility of his forehand;

3. to add to the ease and carriage of the horse and to make him more pleasurable to ride.

In other words, collection is effected and improved by engaging the hind legs, with the joints bent and supple, forward under the horse's body by the use of temporary, but often repeated, action of the seat and legs of the rider, driving the horse forward toward a more or less stationary or restraining hand. Collection is consequently not achieved by shortening the pace through a resisting action of the hand, but instead by using the seat and legs to engage the hind legs further under the horse's body. However, the hind legs should not be engaged too far forward under the horse, as this would shorten the base of support too much, and thereby impede the movement.

On the other hand, a horse whose base of support is too long, will be unable or unwilling to engage his hind legs forward under the body and will never achieve an acceptable collection. Having achieved such collection the horse carries himself well, with lively impulsion, which originates in the activity of the quarters.

The position of the head and neck of a horse at the collected paces is naturally dependent on his stage of training and, in some degree, on his conformation. It should, however, be distinguished by a raised neck, unrestrained and forming a harmonious curve from the withers to the poll (which is the highest point) with the head slightly in front of the vertical. At the moment the rider applies his aids in order to obtain a momentary collecting effect, however, the head may become more or less perpendicular.

The best means to obtain these goals are half-halts as well as the lateral movements, such as travers, renvers and shoulder-in.

Collection means that you gradually shift the horse's center of balance to the rear, thus decreasing the weight on the forehand. Think of a see-saw. When you weigh down one end (bend the

83

joints of the quarters) the other end goes up. Avoid shortening the neck too much. Keep the nose in front of the vertical. The poll must be the highest point. If the neck is shortened too soon and too much it is easy to get false flexion so that a point behind the third neck vertebra becomes the highest one. If the neck is raised by the hands of the rider, it will not be stretched. So ride your horse "short behind" and "long in front."

Engage your horse when he is in motion (not at halts) and, to begin with, only for short periods of time. This work puts a great strain on him and he needs time to muscle up and adjust himself to the increased demands.

The collected trot is developed from the working trot by half-halts and increased driving aids. The trot must retain impulsion and remain brisk and flowing. Dragging or floating, passage type steps are serious faults. The collected trot or collection at the working trot is the foundation for the extended trot.

The collected canter is developed from the working canter by more engagement of the quarters. The liveliness and the rhythm of the canter must be maintained. If the horse shows a tendency to four beat canter, he must be ridden forward in a livelier tempo.

And again a warning against riding at the collected walk for long periods of time.

After every period of collected work, ride your horse freely forward and let him stretch his joints.

THE HALT

At the halt the well schooled horse should stand attentive, motionless and straight, with the weight evenly distributed over all four legs, in pairs abreast of each other. The neck should be raised, the poll high and the head slightly in front of the vertical. The horse may quietly champ the bit, while maintaining a light contact with the rider's hand, and should be ready to move off at the slightest indication of the rider.

The halt is obtained by the displacement of the horse's weight from the forehand to the quarters by a properly increased action of the seat and legs of the rider, driving the horse toward a restraining but allowing hand, causing an almost instantaneous, but not abrupt, halt at a previously fixed place.

Prepare for the halt by half-halts and continue the half-halt into the halt. Lighten up the forehand and do not let him lie on the bit and drop down on the forehand. There is a vast difference between riding to a halt and just ceasing to go forward. To begin with, ride the transition into the halt progressively. Gradually demand more and more, and reduce the number of intermediate steps at canter, trot or walk. Finally, you can break from collected canter or collected trot *directly* to the halt. It takes time. Remember that the horse must remain on the bit and that the transition must be smooth and precise.

Approach the halt with your horse straight and keep him straight at the halt. A crooked halt is a serious fault.

When a horse halts, his hind legs should be well under his body, because of the influence of your seat and legs. As soon as he halts, relax your hands and permit him to correct himself by moving his front legs forward a little. Do not let him creep back. It is a grave fault if the horse steps backward at the halt, especially with both hind legs. Think forward, even at the halt.

The position of the front legs—at least at the lower levels—is more important than the position of the hind legs, because the rider can easily control the position of the front legs. It is more difficult to tell about the position of the hind legs. You must feel it. Make it a habit at the halts to lower your eyes and watch the shoulders and you can tell if the horse is square or not. Do not change your seat, do not stand up in the stirrups and do not lean forward to one side to control the front legs. It is very amateurish and will only disturb your horse and make him upset. Just glance down, do not move your head.

If you find that he is not square in front, his right front leg,

85

for instance, being too far back, you should correct him by moving his right front leg forward. This is done as follows: keep contact with both reins and squeeze with your right lower leg on the girth or behind the elbow of the horse. At the same time, relax your right hand, permitting him to move his right front leg forward. Be ready to resume contact with your right rein to limit the length of the stride. The left rein controls the left front leg and prevents the horse from moving forward.

If you want to move a hind leg forward or sideways, to straighten him squeeze with your lower leg behind the girth.

When you train your horse, you must require him to stand still at halts. After the standstill, make the necessary corrections and let him again stand still. *Never correct him backward.*

Finish every lesson with a good halt.

If you ride a halt in a test (at least at the lower levels) and think that the halt is fairly good, be satisfied and continue your ride. You might mess it up if you start to correct and you will perhaps end up in a worse situation. The stillness or immobility of the horse is also an important criterion by which the judge evaluates a halt. If correcting a minor fault of leg placement or crookedness means that you will be moving or swaying to and fro, you might receive a lower score, even if you succeed in straightening your horse, than you would have if you had accepted the first halt. It is better to move off and work for a high score in the next movement.

The halt and salute is the first and the last movement in the test. It is the judges' first and last impression of your ride. Do not miss this opportunity to impress the judges favourably. You and your horse should look alert and proud. Do not rush. The stopwatch starts when you move off. If you think it is necessary to make a correction, do it quietly, but do not go on forever. Come to a standstill. Salute.

A lady places the reins in her left hand, drops the right hand straight down to her right side and bows her head briefly and graciously. A crisp accurate salute without a change in posture is most effective. Do not overdo the salute.

A gentleman places the reins in his left hand, removes his hat with his right hand by grasping the hatbrim, lowers his right hand with hat in hand to his right side. He must not show the inside of his hat to the judges. Upon replacing his hat, the gentleman must secure it on his head by using the brim only.

At the last halt and salute, the rider should show a pleasant face and smile.

When you have performed the first salute, arrange your reins, *prepare* for the move off (firmer seat) and proceed only when you and your horse are ready. Do not move off without having good control of your horse and yourself. After the salute, do not move your seat out of the saddle and sit down again as if you were saying: now I am ready. At the higher levels the move off must be performed *without* intermediate steps. If you, for instance, proceed from a halt to collected trot, the *first* stride, not the second or third, must be a trotstep. Otherwise you lose valuable points.

THE REIN BACK

The rein back is an equilateral, retrogade movement in which the feet are raised and set down almost simultaneously by diagonal pairs; each forefoot being raised and set down an instant before the diagonal foot, so that, on hard ground, as a rule four separate beats are clearly audible. The feet should be well raised and the hind feet should remain in line.

At the preceding halt, the horse must remain on the bit, maintaining his desire to move forward.

If a trot or a canter is required after a rein back, as in a higher level test, the horse should strike off immediately into this pace without an intermediate step.

Anticipation or precipitation of the movement, any signs of hurrying, resistance to or evasion of the hand, deviation of the

KAY MEREDITH

The Rein Back—The Legs Move in Diagonal Pairs

88

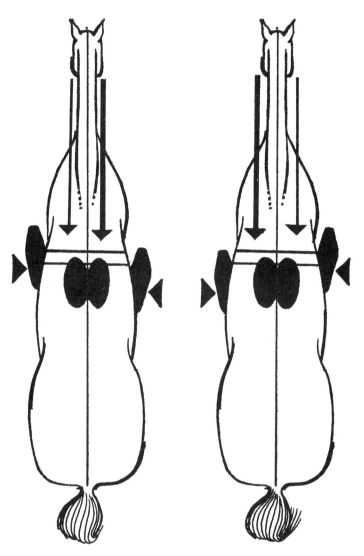

The Aids at the Rein Back—Unilateral Aids

quarters from the straight line, spreading or inactive hind legs, and dragging the forefeet, are all serious faults.

Start to teach the horse the rein back while dismounted. Stand in front of him, one hand on each rein. Use one rein at a time and move him backward, step by step. If he is unwilling, touch him with your toes or the whip on the coronet. When this works, you can mount him.

Walk and then halt, using both legs just behind the girth, with the horse on the bit. Wait a few seconds and control his suppleness. If he resists, the rein back will be very poor. Now use the unilateral aids to start, for instance, with the right rein and right leg. As soon as he obeys by lifting his right hind leg, relax your right hand and squeeze the left rein and left leg, and so on. Because of this regular change between taking and giving, the horse will move the diagonal legs in a steady, walking rhythm.

If he refuses to rein back, he is not on the bit (generally above the bit, whereby the effect of the rein stops in the neck), or his hind feet are stuck to the ground. Ride him forward a few strides, bring him on the bit and try again. If this does not work, move him a stride away from your leg (start a turn on the forehand) and move him backward when the hind leg leaves the ground. As soon as he takes a step backward, reward him. The main thing now is to teach him to go backward. As soon as he understands this, you can straighten him.

It is often useful to dismount and start again from the ground if he refuses to rein back.

If the horse rushes backward or comes behind the bit, tighten your seat and push him forward. Do not lean backward. By leaning backward you make it more difficult for him to use his hind legs.

In the beginning ask your horse just to move backward, but as he progresses, you should ask for a certain number of strides (four, five, six). Count the number of strides by the beat of the front leg. Every step backward with one front leg is considered to be one stride. After the rein back go directly from your last

90

position into the prescribed pace without trying to make the horse square.

At the higher levels you alternatively rein back, go forward and rein back again, which is called the swing. For example, a sequence of 4, 4, 6 steps or 6, 4, 4. This is a good exercise and a good test of his obedience. He should move backward and forward without hesitation at the walk rhythm. He should not be square between the parts of the movement.

If you rein back in the arena at one of the sides, start with the inside aids since you can control the haunches and keep him straight by having the wall or the rail as a help on your outside.

The rein back can be used as a punishment. If the horse runs backward, rein him back until he get tired of it and starts to think forward again.

Common Faults at the Rein Back

The transition into the halt is too abrupt.

The horse is not on the bit with a forward attitude. He moves either above the bit unwillingly, sometimes by jerks and sometimes with dragging feet, or behind the bit, evading the rider's hand.

The rein back is hurried and deviating from the straight line, or with spreading and inactive haunches.

The transition from the rein back into the prescribed pace is ridden with too many intermediate steps.

THE HALF-TURN ON THE HAUNCHES
THE HALF-PIROUETTE AT THE WALK

The half-turn on the haunches is a schooling exercise which is executed from a *medium* walk and is preparatory for the half-pirouette, which is executed at a *collected* walk.

The forehand traces a half-circle around the haunches and moves in even, quiet and regular steps around the horse's inner hind leg, while maintaining the rhythm of the walk. In the half-

KAY MEREDITH
The Half-turn on the Haunches—Look in the Direction You Are Moving.
Feel That You Are Turning Yourself and Taking the Horse With You.

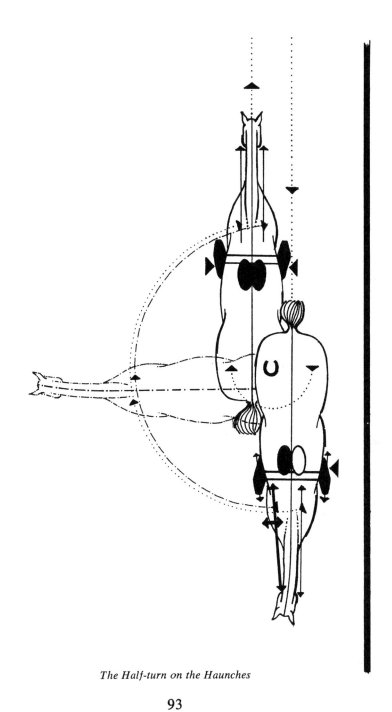

The Half-turn on the Haunches

93

turn, the horse is not required to step with his inside hind leg in the same spot each time it leaves the ground, but may move slightly forward. Backing or loss of rhythm are serious faults. After completion of the turn, the horse walks on without a pause.

The half-pirouette at the walk is a small half-circle on two tracks with a radius equal to the length of the horse, the forehand moving around the haunches. The fore-feet and the outside hind foot move around the inside hind foot, which forms the pivot and should return to the same spot, or slightly in front of it, each time it leaves the ground. The outside hind foot should touch the ground in front of the inside hind foot. During the movement the horse should remain on the bit with a light contact and should maintain his impulsion, and never in the slightest move backward or deviate sideways. If the inside hind foot is not raised and returned to the ground in the same rhythm as the outside hind foot, the pace is no longer regular. The exact rhythm and footfall sequence of the walk must be maintained.

The aids for the half-turn and the half-pirouette are the same. You use diagonal aids, for instance, right rein, left leg.

Prepare for the turn by a half-halt. Sit inward. The inside rein bends the horse slightly and leads the horse, step by step, around the inside hind leg. Your inside leg on the girth maintains the bend and prevents the inside hind leg from falling in. The outside leg moves the horse and prevents the quarters from falling out. The outside rein defines the degree of the bend and, if necessary, supports the outside leg.

Look in the direction you will move, and feel that you are turning yourself and taking the horse with you.

You should lead with the inside rein, rather than pull. It is easy to pull him backward. In the early training of this movement you must use your outside leg firmly, especially during the last part of the turn when it is tempting to the horse to move the haunches out. If necessary, loosen your leg and give the horse a kick, or support the leg with the whip until he obeys without resistance. Do not stop squeezing until you are back on the track. It is easy to lose the last two strides and thus perform a

94

poor turn. If the horse performs a small half-circle, which he will do in the beginning, and if you are one or two strides inside the track, move him *immediately* back to the track at a half-pass or use leg yielding if you cannot keep him bent in the direction of the turn. In this way you correct him, improve his obedience to your outside leg, and gradually decrease the half-circle. Finally, you can turn him, centered around the inside hind foot.

If he steps backward, push him forward with both legs. If he does not maintain the rhythm, is lazy behind, or stuck to the ground, use your legs and your whip with more emphasis. *It is sometimes necessary to move your inside leg backward to keep his inside hind leg active or prevent it from moving inward.* When the horse bends willingly use both of your legs behind the girth. Another way to correct laziness behind is to ride the turn step by step, with a halt between every step.

As a preparation for the half-turn it is useful to ride quarter-turns, turning from one long side to the other. You can turn anywhere on one long side, go across the arena to the other long side, take the right or left rein, walk along the long side a few lengths, and again ride a quarter-turn, and so on. You should try to keep the inside hind leg on the track when you perform the turn.

Another way to develop the half-turn on the haunches is to ride a small half-circle and gradually diminish the size of it.

To perform the half-pirouette, the walk must be collected. The collected walk must remain marching and vigorous, with shorter but more energetic strides. What you lose in length, you gain in elevation. Collect the horse before the half-pirouette and then resume the medium walk, or ride a transition to extended walk after the pirouette.

COMMON FAULTS AT THE HALF-TURN AND THE HALF-PIROUETTE

The horse is not bent in the direction in which he is turning.

The inside foot is not raised and returned to the same spot, but is like a turning screw, stuck or partly stuck to the ground, because of lack of impulsion or not sufficiently engaging aids from the rider.

95

The walk-rhythm is not maintained.

The horse moves backward or deviates sideways with his quarters.

The haunches move on a circle.

Pivoting of the feet and stepping backward are bad faults.

Performing a small half-circle is a lesser fault than stepping backward.

LATERAL WORK AT WALK AND TROT

During the basic training of the horse you have used leg yielding as a preparation for the lateral work in the higher levels where this work should be performed at a *collected* pace with the horse *bent* uniformly from the poll to the tail.

Lateral movements comprise: shoulder-in, haunches-in (travers, head to the wall), haunches-out (renvers, tail to the wall), half-pass* and the counter-change of hand.

The aim of these movements is to:

1. improve obedience to the rider's aids,

2. supple all parts of the horse, thereby increasing the freedom of his shoulders and the suppleness of his quarters, as well as the elasticity of the bond connecting the mouth, the poll, the neck, the back and the haunches,

3. improve cadence and bring balance and pace into harmony,

4. develop and increase engagement of the quarters and thereby also, collection.

As all bending at the poll and neck has a repercussion on the whole spine, the bend must never be exaggerated to such an extent that it impairs the balance and fluency of the movement

---

*The expression half-pass is substituted for the expression on two tracks.

concerned. This applies specially to the half-pass, where the bend should be less than in the shoulder-in.

At all lateral work, the horse should be supple and free from tension. The pace must remain free and regular, maintained by constant impulsion, yet cadenced and balanced.

The lateral work should always be followed by energetic movements straight forward, in order to maintain or increase the impulsion.

Shoulder-in

The horse is slightly bent around the inside leg of the rider. The outside shoulder is placed in front of the inside hindquarter. The horse is looking away from the direction in which he is moving.

Shoulder-in is an excellent schooling exercise and is the most useful of all movements to supple and engage a horse and make him obedient to the aids. It is not only a suppling movement, but also a collecting movement, because at every step the horse must move his inside hind leg underneath his body and place it in front of the outside hind leg, which he is unable to do without lowering his inside hip.

Shoulder-in is developed from leg yielding along the wall. The requirements of engagement and bend are gradually increased. Start to practice the shoulder-in at the walk, a few steps to begin with. When the horse understands your aids, ride shoulder-in mainly at the trot.

Ride your horse correctly through the corner and continue the turn (the curved line) until the forehand is inside the track. Perform a half-halt, apply the aids for shoulder-in and move him along the long side. According to the rules, the angle should be about 30°, which means that the horse moves on *three* tracks when you watch him coming toward you, with the outside front and the inside hind leg on the same track. However, it is advisable to widen this angle slightly (let us call it 3½ track) without

97

Left Shoulder-in—The Horse Moves on Three Tracks

LINDA OLIVER
Left Shoulder-in—The Angle Is a Little Wider. Good Impulsion.
The Horse Is Slightly Overflexed.

99

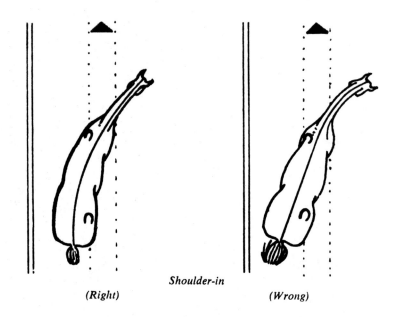

Shoulder-in

(Right)   (Wrong)

aggravating the impulsion—at least when you ride a test. Otherwise it is often hard for the judge to tell if the angle is sufficient.

Apply the inside leg on the girth in order to establish and maintain the bend and to push him forward along the track. Bear down on your inside heel.

The inside rein bends him inward, away from the direction in which he is moving. The inside leg and the inside rein cooperate. The outside leg behind the girth prevents the haunches from falling out. The outside rein controls the bend (limits the bend). If necessary, the outside leg can be used temporarily more forward to influence the outside shoulder. The balance and the collection of the movement is obtained by the use of the outside leg and the outside rein. The more he moves his outside leg forward under the body, the more he must step under with his inside leg to cross in front of the outside leg.

Keep the shoulders sufficiently off the track and keep the haunches on the track. Otherwise, the exercise will be of little value. Maintain the rhythm and the forward movement. Control the impulsion by going across the arena on a single track on a diagonal line, changing the rein, or by riding a circle out of the shoulder-in. Riding a circle is also a means of restoring the bend and the rhythm. On arriving back on the track, go straight forward along the track, or resume the shoulder-in.

The shoulder-in should be ridden with the same bend and the same angle in both directions.

The shoulder-in can also be ridden on the circle. It is a very good exercise to supple your horse and put him to the aids. Ride shoulder-in on the track of the circle or spiral-in (no shoulder-in) and then spiral-out at shoulder-in. The horse should not be overbent. Maintain the same rhythm—do not let him speed up and run away from your aids. He must accept them, and the result should be suppleness and more engagement. Repeat this exercise several times on both reins.

Shoulder-in is a good preparation for the transitions because it makes the horse supple and alert. It is useful to combine shoulder-in with half-halt. Use the circle again. Imagine that you want to strike off from the trot into the canter. Spiral-in at the trot and then out at shoulder-in. Coming back to the track of the circle, ride a half-halt and strike off at the canter. The horse is ready to go and your aids are in the correct position for the departure. In schooling the transition to trot or walk, use a slight shoulder-in at the transition in order to keep him supple and engaged. Later on, when your horse is supple and obedient, you should perform the transitions with an absolutely straight horse.

Shoulder-in is also a good way to prepare for the extensions (see Chapter VI, Transitions and Extensions).

COMMON FAULTS AT THE SHOULDER-IN

The horse's neck is bent too much, often seen when the angle of the movement is too narrow.

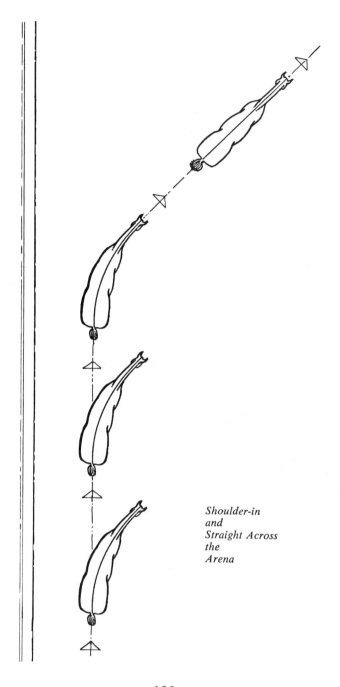

Shoulder-in
and
Straight Across
the
Arena

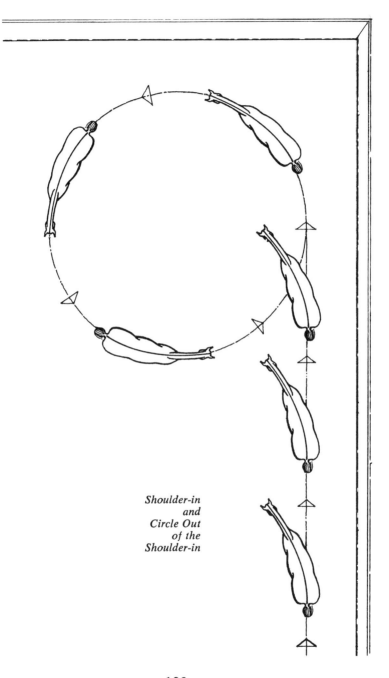

Shoulder-in
and
Circle Out
of the
Shoulder-in

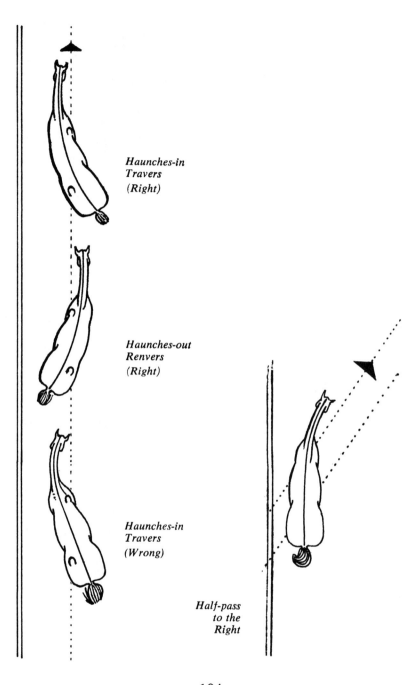

Haunches-in
Travers
(Right)

Haunches-out
Renvers
(Right)

Haunches-in
Travers
(Wrong)

Half-pass
to the
Right

104

The angle is too wide, which impairs the freedom, regularity and harmony of the pace, and restricts the impulsion.

The impulsion is lost because of the rider's preoccupation with bending the horse and pushing him sideways.

The movement is not executed in the same manner on both reins, which also will influence the scoring of the General Impressions under Submission.

Haunches-in (Travers). Haunches-out (Renvers). Half-pass

When executing the *haunches-in,* the horse moves along the wall, being placed obliquely with the head to the wall and the hindquarters to the inside. The horse is slightly bent around the inside leg of the rider. The horse's outside legs pass and cross in front of the inside legs. The horse is looking in the direction in which he is moving.

Travers is performed along the wall or preferably on the center line, at an angle of about 30° to the direction in which the horse is moving. The horse moves on about three tracks.

The *haunches-out* (renvers) is the inverse movement in relation to travers with the tail, instead of the head, to the wall.

Half-pass is a variation of travers, executed on the diagonal instead of along the wall. The horse, slightly bent around the inside leg of the rider, should be as close as possible to being parallel to the long side of the arena, although the forehand should be slightly in advance of the quarters. The outside legs pass and cross in front of the inside legs. The horse should look in the direction in which he is moving. He should maintain the same rhythm and balance throughout the whole movement. In order to give more freedom and mobility to the shoulders, which adds to the ease and grace of the movement, it is of great importance for the horse to be correctly bent, thereby preventing him from protruding his inside shoulder, and also to maintain the impulsion, especially the engagment of the inside leg.

Before these movements are started, the horse must be supple

105

ELIZABETH LEWIS
*Half-pass to the Right—The Horse Is Moving to the Right, Left Legs
Passing and Crossing in front of the Right Legs*

106

*Half-pass to the Left—The Horse Is Moving to the Left, Right Legs
Passing and Crossing in Front of the Left Legs*

and obedient to the unilateral aids. If there is resistance, it will become worse when the diagonal aids are applied (the horse bent in the direction he moves).

The principles and the aids for these movements are the same. It is important to maintain the forward drive or impulsion. It gives brilliance to the movement, especially to the half-pass. Think forward-sideways, not sideways-forward.

The movements should first be carried out sufficiently at the walk, but later on mainly ridden at the trot.

The aids:

Both legs push forward. The inside aids maintain the bend of the horse. It is wrong to overbend him. He should *look* in the direction in which he moves. The neck should not be bent more than the body. The rider's outside leg moves the horse sideways and the outside rein controls the bend. Here again the unilateral aids are useful. If the horse is a little dull to the outside leg, the outside rein should support the leg *without changing the bend*. The rider sits inward, following the horse in the direction in which he moves.

The bend should be about the same at the haunches-in, haunches-out and half-pass.

Transitions from one of these movements to another develops suppleness and teaches the horse to react quickly to the rider's aids. To begin with, the rider should go straight forward a few strides between the transitions. When the horse is more experienced, the transitions can be done directly. The transitions must be smooth.

At the transition from shoulder-in to haunches-in the horse is called to attention by a half-halt, whereupon the forehand is moved back to the track by the outside leading rein. The haunches are moved in by the outside leg. The bend should never change.

At the transition from haunches-in to shoulder-in the horse is ridden forward on a curved line. When the hind feet reach the track a half-halt is performed and the horse is moved forward along the wall at the shoulder-in. The bend should never change.

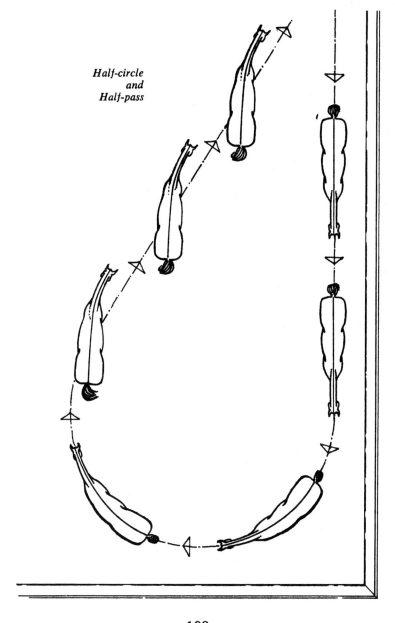

Half-circle
and
Half-pass

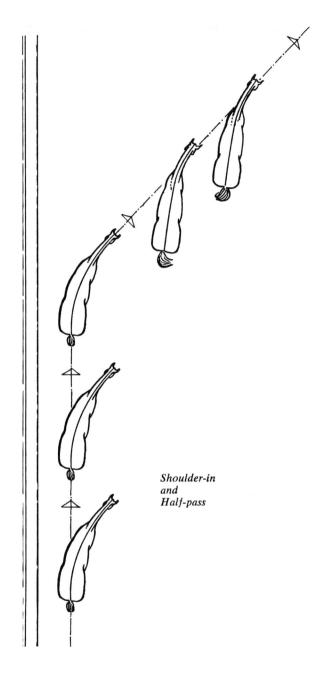

*Shoulder-in
and
Half-pass*

110

Haunches-out can be developed from shoulder-in by changing the aids and the bend. The angle to the wall remains the same. Another way is to ride a half-circle at a half-pass and, just before the long side, check the forehand and move the haunches out to the track. Transitions from shoulder-in to haunches-out are useful if the horse has a tendency to overbend or to fall on the outside shoulder.

The *half-pass* is included in most of the national higher level tests and in all FEI tests.

There are several ways to develop the half-pass. The main problem is to establish the bend and maintain it. However, the foundations is laid by leg yielding across the diagonal. When he "floats" in a supple and obedient way, he is gradually bent in the direction in which he moves. It is better to postpone the bend than to obtain it at the cost of destroying the movement. Start at the walk.

One way to develop the half-pass is to ride a half-circle or half-volte and then take him back to the long side at a half-pass (see picture).

Another way is to start at the shoulder-in along the long side to establish the bend; switch the pressure of the inside leg over to the outside leg; and ride the horse a few strides diagonally toward the center line (see picture). As soon as you lose the bend, straighten the horse, go forward and start again at the next long side.

At the walk you can later on ride a half-pass across the diagonal to the center line; perform a half-turn on the haunches (pirouette) on the center line; and go back at a half-pass to the point on the long side where you started. The purpose of this exercise is to maintain the same rhythm and the same bend from the beginning to the end.

When riding the half-pass across the diagonal, or partly across, pass the corner first before you start. In preparation for riding the half-pass across, or partly across, the diagonal, get well into the corner before you start. Imagine that there is a tree in the

111

corner which you must go around before you start the movement. Otherwise the haunches will probably lead at the half-pass. *You* start (not the horse)—the horse should not anticipate you. Remember that the shoulders of the horse must lead slightly. If you start at the corner, the haunches will probably lead, which is a serious fault. He should be as close as possible to being parallel to the long side. The haunches should neither lead nor trail.

A counterchange means that when riding a half-pass you change the direction and the bend. In many tests you ride half a diagonal at a half-pass, a counterchange at X and a half-pass back to the long side. Imagine that you are on the right rein. To prevent the haunches from leading in the new direction at the counterchange, which is a common and serious fault, you must make him straight for a fraction of a second before the change. In fact the change is performed almost directly, but if the haunches are dragging before the change, they will lead after the change. Begin the change with a soft squeeze of the incoming inside left rein, immediately followed by a squeeze of your incoming outside right leg. Do not change the position of your

EXAMPLE OF A ZIG-ZAG

The first and the last two tracks are of three meters to the right, the three others of six meters.

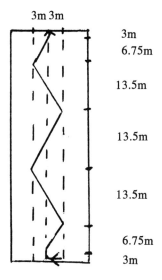

3m 3m

3m
6.75m

13.5m

13.5m

13.5m

6.75m
3m

left leg until you have changed the bend to the left. Use the rein first, then the leg, but the interval is very short.

The zig-zag includes several short half-passes to either side of the center line and counterchanges between them. The size of the zig-zag is described in the actual test. For this specific movement you should concentrate on making the changes smooth, correct (no leading haunches), fluid and precise.

When practicing the zig-zag it is useful to figure out the size in meters and make some sort of mark in the arena so that you become familiar with the requirements and are able to perform it symmetrically, observing the number of meters or strides to either side prescribed in the test.

COMMON FAULTS AT THE HALF-PASS

The horse is too straight or even bent the wrong way (away from the direction in which he moves).

He is not nearly parallel to the long side, and the quarters are either leading or dragging.

He is not uniformly bent to both sides (less to the stiff side).

At changes of direction he anticipates the rider, resulting in the haunches leading.

The lightness, balance and harmony is lost because of lack of impulsion or because of a hurried pace (this is a collected pace, remember).

The rider sits to the outside, collapsing the inside hip.

TRANSITIONS AND EXTENSIONS

The changes of pace and speed should be clearly shown at the prescribed marker; they should be quickly made, yet must be smooth and not abrupt. The rhythm of a pace should be maintained up to the moment when the pace is changed or the horse halts. The horse should remain light in hand, calm and in a correct position. He must be *straight*.

113

The same applies to transitions from one movement to another, for instance from the passage to the extended trot, from the passage to the piaffer and vice versa.

At the higher levels a transition from the halt into trot or canter and vice versa must be executed without intermediate steps at the walk or trot. Intermediate. steps will lower the score.

The horse's ability to perform transitions must be developed gradually, with higher and higher demands until the rider can execute them directly *without intermediate steps.* For instance, trot-halt-trot, canter-halt-canter, piaffer-extended trot-piaffer. The half-halt is the key to all transitions. The horse should be like a *rubber-band,* which can be lengthened and shortened without resistance. Laziness should not be tolerated. After each transition to another pace the harmonious rhythm (cadence) must be established as soon as possible, without hesitation. At the transition to the walk, for instance, the rider must immediately urge the horse forward into a marching walk.

The transitions reveal the truth about the training of the horse. If the rider can send him on and bring him back to hand in a supple and quick way, with good engagement of the quarters, he should be satisfied, knowing that he has done a good job.

Repeated transitions will result in the horse performing the extensions on his own. The extension includes two transitions, one into the extension and one back. Ideally, a good extension across the diagonal should last from marker to marker, demonstrating that the rider can extend quickly and smoothly without an explosion and bring the horse back to hand in one stride.

In training for extensions the horse must understand that he must shift the center of gravity backward so he can move his shoulders freely and stretch the fore legs forward. A good way to reach this goal is by frequent half-halts and shoulder-ins. Because of the engagement, the horse comes off the ground and the suspension is prolonged. It gives him more time to lift the shoulders, stretch the fore-legs and bend the hind legs before they touch the ground again. Through this mechanism the number of strides is not increased, but the horse covers more ground.

This is the reason why the rider must be able to ride at least a moderately collected trot before he asks the horse to extend.

The horse cannot place his fore-legs further forward than the vertical line from the nose. That is the reason why he must have sufficient freedom of his head during extensions. *He must lower and lengthen his neck* to be able to reach forward.

If the horse is supple and engaged he can "float" out with longer strides in the same rhythm on a light contact, and the rider can sit comfortably without bouncing. If he is tense, the extension will be a sudden abrupt effort of his muscles, resulting in a cramped stretching, irregularity and lack of rhythm (running trot). A tense extension can also be caused by the rider who pulls too much, preventing the horse from lengthening the frame.

Consequently, you must supple your horse before you extend. You cannot force him into the extension. Work him on the circle (use shoulder-in) and lengthen the strides along the long side. If he resists when you ask him to come back to hand, take him on the circle again and so on.

LENDON GRAY   *Lengthening the strides at the trot*

In the lower level tests you *lengthen the strides*. This means that when the horse is performing the working trot, he should be able to lengthen his strides without rushing. How much? That is not indicated in the test. However, the main thing is that the strides become longer and the rhythm remains the same. Try to emphasize the transition. If you have a talented horse, which can lengthen in a correct way so that the pace is almost an extended trot, the judge will probably not score you very low.

To begin with, ask only for a few longer strides. At every phase of the training, try to recognize when the horse has reached his peak. Being too ambitious with your pushing aids will result in irregularity, tension or a break to the canter. Ride rising working trot without rushing, even a little slowly to give the horse time to lengthen the strides at the same time that you increase the drive from behind. You can place your weight a little backward. If he speeds up, leans heavily on the bit or "dives" with his head, check him with the rein. He should lengthen his frame, but he must remain on light contact.

If he forges, the trot is generally hurried; or check the shoeing. If he breaks to the canter, correct immediately with the inside rein and leg and push him forward again.

LINDA ZANG   *Lengthening the Strides at the Canter*

The extended trot demonstrates the utmost impulsion attainable and the driving influence of the rider's aids. The horse should be taught to accept the aids for extension willingly.

Keep your hands low and steady so the horse can take a slightly firmer contact. Full development of impulsion is impossible without contact. The contact, however, must never deteriorate into leaning on the hand. Since a good extension depends on the engagement of the quarters, you should prepare for the extension with a half-halt. When you are training the horse, you can also ride shoulder-in along the short side and extend along the long side.

Ride extended trot for a short period of time only. It is a demanding exercise.

The canter extensions are executed on the same principles.

COMMON FAULTS AT MEDIUM TROT

Too feeble (lack of hock action, freedom of shoulders and balance) or too powerful, resembling the extended trot.

Running with short steps, unsettled and irregular.

COMMON FAULTS AT EXTENDED TROT

The transition into extended trot is too explosive and the transition back to hand is too abrupt or not smooth.

The head is too high, the neck too short, resulting in a constrained action with locked shoulders, foreleg movements too high (often flicking of the forelegs) and dragging hind legs, the shinbones of which are not parallel with those of the forelegs. The forefeet do not touch the ground on the spot toward which they are pointing but rather behind this point.

The trot is an irregular running trot with short steps, lacking the elasticity which comes from a supple back.

COMMON FAULTS AT MEDIUM CANTER

Too slack (lack of hock action) or too powerful, sometimes prejudicial to balance and calmness.

Irregular, due to a high head, a "dead" back and therefore trailing hind legs.

Not straight along straight lines.

Not straight at the transition back to collected canter or working canter.

117

Too slack or "nervous," or too fast because of an increasing frequency of short strides, instead of a marked lengthening of every stride.

Not straight along straight lines or at the transition back to collected canter.

The transition into extended canter is too explosive. The horse is not given the opportunity to develop the activity of his quarters and the maximum length of the strides while maintaining the calmness, rhythm and light contact.

The transition from the extended to the collected canter is not straight, or disunited or on the forehand, the horse heavy on the bit because of the rider using heavy hands instead of half-halts.

THE FLYING CHANGE

The change of leg is executed in close connection with the suspension which follows each stride of the canter. Flying changes of leg can also be executed in series, for instance at every 4th, 3rd, 2nd and at every stride. The horse, even in series, remains light, calm and straight, with lively impulsion, maintaining the same rhythm and balance throughout the series concerned. In order not to restrict or restrain the lightness and fluency of the flying changes of leg in series, the degree of collection should be slightly less than otherwise at collected canter.

At the change in series of every 4th stride, the leading front leg touches the ground four times before the change, at the every 3rd, three times, at the every 2nd, twice, and at every stride, once.

The aids of the rider should be as discreet as possible.

Let us suppose that you are riding right lead canter and perform a flying change to left lead canter. The horse changes the position of the legs in the air. Instead of setting the left hind leg down, he sets the right hind leg down and continues with the other legs in the left lead canter. He changes first with the hind legs and immediately afterward with the front legs. However, watching a horse one has the impression that he changes the hind legs and the front legs at the same time.

The success of the flying change depends on the timing of aids.

The aids must be given immediately before the suspension when the leading front leg touches the ground.

Imagine that you are riding right lead canter and want to change to left lead canter. Before the change, move your right leg back to a position behind the girth, so that it is on the right spot when you give the signal for the change—a squeeze with your right leg. Otherwise the signal will probably come too late. It is a help to count every time the front leg touches the ground, for instance one, two, three, four. On four, you squeeze with your right leg by lowering your heel and take a short pull on the right rein. The pull tells the horse to set his right hind leg down first. The pull is followed by a relaxation of your hand and you switch the horse softly over to the left rein.

If the horse thinks forward at the canter, your left leg has nothing to do with the change. Move it to the girth, keep it there and do not let it slide forward in an exaggerated way. If the horse has a tendency to swing the haunches to the left, keep your left leg behind the girth. Keep your body quiet. Do not look down.

This seems very simple, but do not expect success the first time you try the flying change. It will take some time, less with a talented horse with a good canter, longer with horses with a poor canter. The success, however, depends on

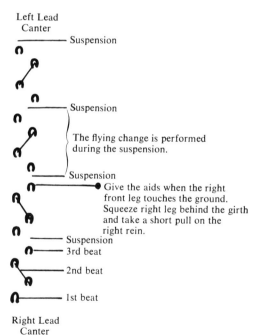

Left Lead
Canter

Suspension

Suspension

The flying change is performed during the suspension.

Suspension

Give the aids when the right front leg touches the ground. Squeeze right leg behind the girth and take a short pull on the right rein.

Suspension

3rd beat

2nd beat

1st beat

Right Lead
Canter

The flying change from right to left lead canter.

119

the preparations you have made. Before you start the flying changes the horse must be absolutely obedient to your aids for the departure into canter, and he must be in good balance and reliable at the counter-canter. He must respond easily to your aids when you ask him to increase or decrease the tempo.

A good preparation for the flying change is what can be called a quick change of lead. Cantering, for instance, on the right lead, you break the canter and immediately pick up the other lead. You reduce the interval between the right lead and the left lead to a minimum. When he performs the quick change easily, you can start the flying change.

The quality of the change depends on the quality of the canter at the moment of the change. If the canter lacks impulsion, if the horse resists or is upset, bring him patiently back to harmony before you change. Many horses get upset at this work, but the only way to solve this problem is to make your horse calm before you try again.

A good way to teach the flying change is to change from counter-canter to true canter on the circle. You can also ride a half-circle and change upon the return to the long side, or change from one big circle to the other, or change the rein across the diagonal with a flying change at the end of the diagonal.

If you practice one of these methods, and the horse starts to anticipate you, use one of the others.

When the horse performs the changes on these curved lines, you should practice the flying changes along straight lines. The goal is to perform the flying changes with the horse perfectly straight.

At the changes, it is important that the horse "jumps through," i.e. that the hind leg goes well forward under the body. In the beginning, the horse will often prop both hind legs down at the same time, or he is late behind, which means that he changes first in front and then behind. If these faults appear, you must increase the effect of the squeezing leg. If necessary, support your leg with the whip.

It is useful to have a knowledgeable person on the ground who can tell you about the hind leg if you do not feel it. The late change behind is often hard to eliminate if the horse has made it a habit.

If you intend to practice the flying changes, start the lesson while the horse is fresh and work him for a fairly short period of time. When the single change is stabilized, the changes in series can begin.

At changes in series every fourth stride, count on the front leg—one, two, three, four and give the aids to change on four. In every third, you give the aids on three, in every second on two. At every second stride you do not have time to move your lower legs. You will be too late with your aids. Keep both your legs in the same position behind the girth.

At the changes at every stride, you must be very alert to be on time with the aids. Start with two changes. At the right lead, for instance, change to the left and immediately back to the right. As soon as the left front leg begins to touch the ground, give the aids for the change. You can ride this exercise either on a big circle changing to counter-canter and back to true canter, or along a straight line. The next step is to ride three changes along a straight line, which generally does not cause any problems. The problems arise when you ask for four or five changes. The horse gets upset because of the frequent leg aids or because you cannot follow him and thus disturb the rhythm. After long training, however, the changes at every stride will be like a pace.

Change of direction on curved lines in connection with a flying change (for instance figure of eight, serpentine) is easier to perform smoothly and fluently if the horse is straight at the change. At the intersection of the circles or when crossing the center line, you should therefore make your horse straight for a length.

COMMON FAULTS AT THE FLYING CHANGES

The movement lacks impulsion and is therefore not sufficiently fluent, free, supple and straight.

The shoulders are constrained and the quarters swinging.

The canter is hurried.

Both hind feet are together at the change or the hind foot changes a moment after the fore feet.

121

The horse omits one or two changes in a series, or executes them at a wrong sequence, or produces too many or too few changes.

The horse is on his forehand (the croup too high, the joints not bent), "dives" and does not gain enough ground.

The aids of the rider are too noticeable and brusque (for instance, hands too hard and jerking), The upper body leaning forward, the seat out of the saddle and the legs flailing and kicking the horse.

HALF-PASS AT THE CANTER

The principles, the aids and the requirements for the half-pass at the canter are the same as for the half-pass at the trot. The horse looks in the direction in which he moves. The rhythm and the floating movement forward generated by a lively impulsion must be maintained. The shoulders should be slightly in advance and the haunches should neither lead nor drag with the horse being almost parallel to the long side.

Start to ride the horse away from the long side at a half-pass for a few strides, then make him straight and go forward. Gradually increase the number of strides until you reach the center line. You can also ride a half-circle and go back to the long side at a half-pass. When this works, you add a flying change on the center line or upon the return to the long side after the half-circle. Straighten your horse before the change. Finally, you can ride a half-pass across the whole diagonal with a flying change at the long side before the corner.

Now you can begin with more demanding exercises, the counter change and the zig-zag. At the counter change you ride half a diagonal to X, perform a flying change when you change the direction and the bend and ride a half-pass back to the long side. Prepare for the counter change with a half-halt without losing the rhythm. Do not let him anticipate, do not let him lean on the bit, and use your aids in the same way as at the trot to prevent the haunches from leading.

The zig-zag consists of several half-passes and counter changes across the center line. The number of half-passes varies, depend-

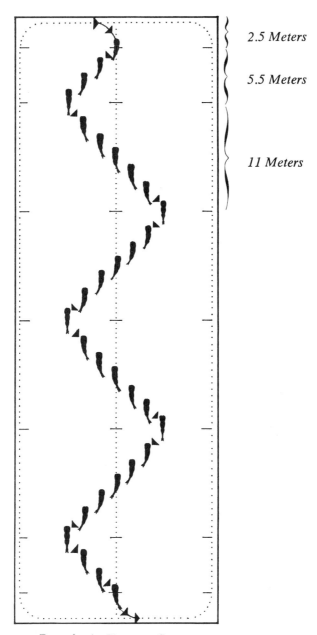

2.5 Meters

5.5 Meters

11 Meters

Example of a Zig-zag at Canter

123

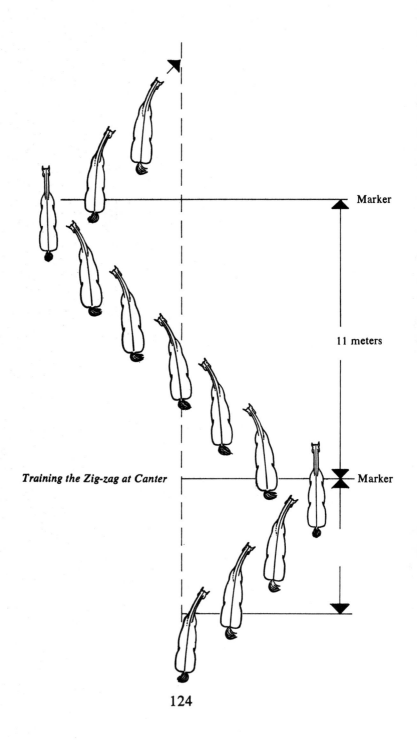

Marker

11 meters

Training the Zig-zag at Canter

Marker

ing on the degree of difficulty of the test. Each half-pass should be the same size, and the horse should gain ground in the same number of strides (meters) forward and sideways.

For instance, a zig-zag consisting of four half-passes with four strides, eight strides, eight strides and four strides, is fairly easy.

A zig-zag shown in the drawing with half-passes of three and six strides is a difficult movement. The length of the center line is 60 meters. You must figure out how much room you have at your disposal for every half-pass and then adjust the strides and the angle of the half-pass to the space disposable. In this example, the horse has to perform two short and four long half-passes. You need some meters at the turn down the center line and some at the end to make the horse straight. This means that you can move forward only 11 meters in one long half-pass.

First ride some counter changes at every sixth stride. Give the aids when the leading front leg touches the ground for the sixth time. It is important that you start the next half-pass immediately, otherwise you lose valuable ground and you will be in trouble at the zig-zag.

Put some markers on the ground for 11 meters and try to ride a half-pass of six strides within this limited area. When this works, you can start practicing the zig-zag.

THE HALF-PIROUETTE AND THE PIROUETTE AT CANTER

In the pirouette, the forehand moves around the haunches, maintaining the exact cadence and sequence of legs of the canter. The inside hind leg forms the pivot and should return to the same spot each time it leaves the ground. The rider should maintain perfect lightness while accentuating the collection and engagement of the quarters. In the half-pirouette the horse is turned 180°, and in the pirouette it is 360°. In the half-pirouette he should execute three to four strides, in the pirouette six to eight.

A pirouette demands a very high degree of collection. It is a canter on the spot. The pirouette starts when the forward movement ceases along the straight line.

ELIZABETH LEWIS
The Pirouette at Canter—The Beginning of the Pirouette

JOHN WINNETT
The Pirouette at Canter—The Pirouette Starts When the Forward Movement Ceases. The Rider Sits Inward

127

DOROTHY MORKIS

The Pirouette at Canter—The Horse Is Lively and Energetic With the Haunches Well Engaged, the Croupe Lowered and the Forehand Elevated, the Tail, However Is Swishing.

LINDA ZANG   *The Pirouette at Canter*

128

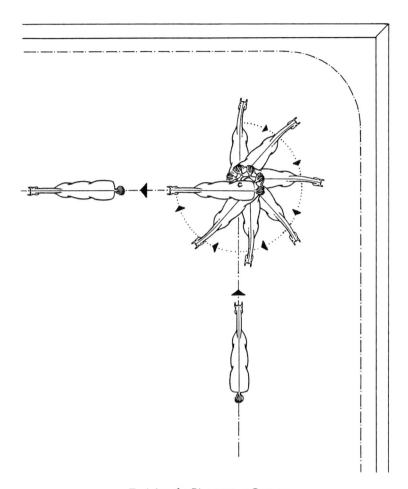

Training the Pirouette at Corners

The principles and the aids for the pirouette at the canter are the same as for the pirouette at the walk. Establish a correct rhythm with good engagement so he can "sit" at the pirouette with well bent joints. He must be supple. If he is tense, he will probably whirl around above the bit. Sit inward. Look in the direction you turn and take the horse with you. Both legs behind

129

the girth maintain the canter, keeping the hind legs active. The inside leg maintains the bend in cooperation with the inside rein and prevents the haunches from falling in. It is a common fault that the inside hind foot moves inward at the first stride of the pirouette. The outside leg moves the horse around and prevents the haunches from falling out. The inside rein leads the horse into the turn (do not pull him backward). The outside rein controls the bend and supports the outside leg.

After the last stride, make the horse straight and continue the canter at the same rhythm. Do not let him rush or "catapult" out of the pirouette.

In some tests you ride half a diagonal to X, where you perform a half-pirouette. The horse must be *straight* on the diagonal. It is very tempting to prepare for the half-pirouette by riding the diagonal at a half-pass, which is incorrect. After the pirouette, restore the impulsion and push the horse slightly forward in order to get a fluid forward flying change.

When schooling your horse at pirouettes, start with a half-volte followed by a half-pass either along the long side or on the diagonal. Gradually decrease the half-volte on which the hind feet move until the inside hind foot moves on the spot.

Another good exercise is to work on a circle and decrease it more and more. The rider can always control or restore the impulsion and the rhythm by going forward, increasing the circle.

Now the pirouettes should be performed along a straight line. One good way is to use the corners of the arena as a help. Ride counter canter about two horse lengths inside the track. When you approach the short side, collect the horse and perform a ¾-pirouette toward the wall, make him straight, continue at the counter-canter and ride another pirouette at the next or second next corner (see picture).

You should now be ready to practice the pirouettes on the diagonal or on the center line.

COMMON FAULTS AT THE PIROUETTE

The impulsion, cadence and regular sequence of the legs are

not maintained; the horse spins around, executing only a few strides at a tense and hurried canter.

The horse is not bent to the direction in which he is turning.

The inside hind foot is not raised and returned to the same spot or almost to the same spot, or it moves inward the first stride.

The haunches move on a circle which, however, is a lesser fault than being stuck to the ground, losing the rhythm of the canter.

The horse moves backward (a serious fault).

The canter is sometimes disunited, the horse changing the leg, often only for a fraction of a second and solely with his hind legs.

The horse is not collected or straight enough when cantering up to the spot where the pirouette is supposed to be executed.

The quarters deviate to the inside or to the outside.

The transition out of the pirouette is too explosive.

THE PIAFFER

The piaffer demands the highest degree of collection and is required only in the most advanced tests. The piaffer is a highly measured, collected, elevated and cadenced trot on the spot. The horse's back is supple and vibrating. The quarters are slightly lowered, the haunches with active hocks are well engaged, giving great freedom, lightness and mobility to the shoulders and the forehand. Each diagonal pair of feet is raised and returned to the ground alternately, with an even rhythm and a slightly prolonged suspension.

The neck should be raised and arched, the head perpendicular. The horse should remain light on the bit with a supple poll, maintaining a light contact on a taut rein. The body of the horse should move up and down in a supple, cadenced and harmonious movement (the horse should bounce) without swinging either the forehand or the quarters from one side to the other.

131

The Piaffer

In principle, the height of the toe of the raised foreleg should be level with the middle of the cannon bone of the supporting foreleg. The toe of the raised hind leg should be slightly lower, reaching just above the fetlock joint of the supporting hind leg.

The piaffer, although being executed on the spot, must be animated by a lively impulsion which is displayed in the horse's constant desire to move forward as soon as the aids calling for the piaffer cease.

Before teaching the piaffer the horse must be in absolute balance and able to perform a well collected trot with smooth transition into extended trot and back to collected trot. The trot must be characterized by a lively impulsion which is a condition for the piaffer.

HILDA GURNEY

*The Piaffer—Expression of Energy. The Croupe Is Lowered,
the Forehand Elevated*

It is advisable to start with the piaffer, not the passage, because
it is easier at the piaffer to teach the horse to bend his joints.

The piaffer can be taught under the rider or by work in hand.
It is generally easier to start to work the horse in hand and then
mount him.

If you prefer to teach the piaffer from the saddle, you must
create an impulsion, which you check. The forward urge must
always be present. Sit deep in the saddle and tighten your seat.
Start along the wall (the wall helps you to keep the horse *straight*)
with transitions within the collected trot, and gradually shorten the
strides until the horse moves forward about a hoof's length. It is
important to reward him as soon as he takes some short steps.
Bring him to a halt and relax.

133

At this work it is useful to have an assistant with a long whip used behind the girth, or just above the hocks, or touching the horse lightly on the shin-bones if he is dragging his hind legs. The touch of the whip should come when the hind foot touches the ground which will tell the horse to raise the foot quicker and bend his joints more. However, you should never become dependent on the assistant. You are on your own when you have entered the arena at a show.

As the training develops, the assistant should only raise the whip without touching the horse, and as soon as possible you work on your own.

You must *proceed slowly*. When the piaffer becomes irregular, ride forward at the trot. Double steps and swinging of the forehand or the haunches outward, generally is an indication that the piaffer has been executed on the spot too soon.

Ideally the horse should start the piaffer when you ask for it and continue on his own until you ask for something else. A constant tapping of the legs and moving of the seat should be avoided.

The work in hand should be performed along a wall on a straight line. Pass the corners at the walk. In the beginning you will need an assistant. The horse should be equipped with a snaffle and a cavesson with side reins attached as for longeing. A longeline or a leading rein is attached to the cavesson. To begin with, the assistant handles the leading rein and you are in charge of the whip which represents the pushing aids. But as soon as possible you should try to handle both the leading rein and the whip. To start with, lead the horse around the arena at the walk. Then urge him into a collected trot with the whip and clicks of your tongue. Do not permit him to lean on the bit or to rush. Gradually by more influence (more restriction) of the leading rein and more pushing forward by the whip and clicks of your tongue, you will have some steps at the piaffer. At the piaffer, *let him always move forward a little.* Keep the horse *straight.* If he is crooked, the assistant should move the shoulders slightly inward by the leading rein. If the forelegs hardly leave the

Work in Hand
*Instructor and Assistant—The Horse Should Start the Piaffer When the
Instructor Raises the Whip*

Rider Up to Get the Horse Used to the Weight of the Rider at the Piaffer

135

Instructor Supports the Rider

The Final Result—The Rider on Her Own

136

Work in Hand in the Snaffle Only

ground, touch him with the whip above the knee of the foreleg. The horse should develop such an attention to the aids that you just have to raise the whip to start the piaffer. When you lower the whip the horse should stop. After a while, you can start the piaffer from the walk or from the halt.

The horse should now be saddled. It is useful to put a rider on him to get him used to the weight of the rider at the piaffer.

When the horse works well in the cavesson, you take over the leading rein and pretty soon you can work him alone in the snaffle only.

If you are on the left rein, keep your left hand on the mane (you are facing the horse), the inside left rein under the little finger coming back between the long finger and the index, the outside right rein between the inner joint of the index and the thumb, which rests flat on the rein. The right hand handles the whip.

As the work proceeds, you can begin the lesson (not every day) by work in hand for a few minutes and then mount him and practice the piaffer. It is useful, in the beginning and sometimes later on, to have an assistant on the ground.

COMMON FAULTS AT THE PIAFFER

The horse is above the bit with his head too much in front of the perpendicular, with a hollow back resulting in an insufficient elevation of the knees with straight inactive haunches.

The horse is behind the bit with evasion of the hand, often with the forelegs and the hind legs raised and put down too close to each other with a base that is too narrow.

The pace is irregular, as the horse, in order to maintain his balance, is more or less forced to take double steps with his hind legs or he swings his front legs and/or his hind legs outward or crosses his front legs in a weaving way.

The piaffer is too earthbound without suspension.

The horse stiffens his front legs against the movement and executes a piaffer lacking impulsion.

The horse moves backward (grave fault) or forward.

The quarters (the croup) are too high.

The horse does not perform the prescribed number of steps. For instance seven steps instead of 10-12 must be scored as insufficient.

THE PASSAGE

The passage is a measured, very collected, very elevated and very cadenced trot. It is required only in the most advanced dressage tests. It is characterized by a pronounced engagement of the quarters, a more accentuated flexion of the knees and hocks, and a graceful elasticity of the movement. Each diagonal pair of legs is raised and returned to the ground alternately, gaining little ground and with an even cadence and a prolonged suspension. In principle, the height of the toe of the raised foreleg should be level with the middle of the cannon bone of the other foreleg. The toe of the raised hind leg should be slightly above the fetlock joint of the other hind leg.

LINDA ZANG   *The Passage*

ELIZABETH LEWIS   *The Passage*
More engagement of the hindquarters desirable

139

JOHN WINNETT   *The Passage*
*The nose is slightly behind the vertical. The poll should be
the highest point of the neck*

DOROTHY MORKIS   *The Passage*

140

The neck should be raised and gracefully arched with the poll as the highest point and the head close to the perpendicular. The horse should remain light on the bit and be able to go smoothly from the passage into piaffer and vice versa, without apparent effort and without altering the rhythm, the impulsion remaining active and pronounced.

The same passage cannot be expected of all horses. Depending upon conformation and temperament, as well as upon the energy derived from the impulsion, some horses have a more rounded and longer action, others a more lively and shorter action.

The passage can be taught from the walk, the piaffer or the collected trot. Since the trot and the piaffer have more impulsion, it is generally better to start from them.

If the horse works correctly at the piaffer, you have laid a good foundation for the passage, because you have taught him to bend his joints.

At the work in hand you can urge him forward into the passage, and you have to run slowly or walk with long strides to follow him. He must remain light and he should not rush. ·

When riding him, you produce the piaffer and go forward into the passage, trying to maintain the same engagement of the quarters. Increase the pressure of your legs and give a little with your hands. As soon as he takes some floating steps, reward him. If he goes too fast out of the piaffer, you have to check him with the rein by short, repeated pulls. He generally flattens out at the same time and you lose the engagement. If he takes a shorter step with one leg, you must increase the influence of your leg on the same side.

Depending on the temperament of the horse, it is sometimes easier to start from the collected trot and develop it into the passage.

An assistant is helpful. His aid with the whip, however, must coincide with your aids. When you ask for the passage, he must attentively use the whip at the same time. He can also help you to improve the action of the front legs by touching the horse above the knee (the knee meets the whip on its way up). The action of the front legs gives the passage much of its brilliance. If the horse raises his front legs almost to a right angle, it takes more time, prolonges the suspension and improves the cadence.

COMMON FAULTS AT THE PASSAGE

The horse does not maintain a regular, diagonal pace.

The horse takes double steps to maintain his balance.

The horse leans heavily on the bit, with the head too high or too low. If the head is too high, the back is lowered and hollow, resulting in an insufficient raising of the knees and inactive trailing quarters.

The front legs cross over each other, the forehand or the quarters swing from one side to the other (serious fault).

TRANSITIONS IN CONNECTION WITH THE PIAFFER AND THE PASSAGE

In the tests, you perform transitions from the walk into the passage or the piaffer, from the passage into the piaffer and vice versa, from the passage into the extended trot and from the passage into the collected canter. Sometimes, but very seldom, the test includes a transition from the halt into the piaffer.

All transitions must be smooth, calm and quickly made. Prepare for them carefully. At the transition from the piaffer to the passage and vice versa, the cadence must be maintained without effort. The horse often goes into a lower "gear" when going into the piaffer and into a higher one when going out of it. Another fault to be avoided is what can be called "progressive piaffer," which means that the transition is prolonged and lacks precision, resulting in a movement between the piaffer and the passage.

142

You have already ridden the transition from the piaffer to the passage when you developed the passage from the piaffer. The transition from the passage to the piaffer is a real test of the suppleness of the horse. The effect of the rein must go through the body without any resistance. Your seat and legs maintain the impulsion, the elevation and the energy of the steps and your hands decrease the forward movement by repeated actions until he starts the piaffer. The cadence remains the same.

The transition from the passage to the extended trot will not offer any special problems, because the horse has a lot of impulsion. Just be careful to make the transition smooth, keeping the horse on the bit and avoiding an explosion.

At the transition from the walk or the halt you have very little or no impulsion at all to help you. Therefore, before the transition you must prepare him and feel that the horse is very alert and attentive to your aids.

Chapter VII

RIDING HORSES WITH BAD HABITS

The cause of bad habits is generally wrong handling and training of the horse. Try first to find out the reason for his disobedience. Is he just mischievous or is he frightened, in pain, or do you face a deeply rooted disobedience? The disobedience always shows up in the same way. The horse does not go forward willingly and he does not lean in the same way on both reins. He must be suppled and straightened. Riding cross-country in a lively tempo is a good way to make him go forward and accept the bit.

A horse ridden for a long time *above the bit* escapes the influence of the rider's legs, hollows his back and raises his head. The contact between the rider's legs and hands must be restored or established. His head must be lowered, he must stretch into the bit until he can arch his back and use his quarters. You know from the training of the young horse that every horse, sooner or later, will supple if you ride him forward on curved lines, bending him properly. This procedure may take a long time with an "old criminal." Try this: take him on a circle at the walk. Start on the soft side, generally the right. Ride him a little away from your inside aids, (for instance, right shoulder-in or leg yielding) with the forehand slightly inside the track of the circle. The purpose is to lower his head. If he does not yield to your leg, give him a kick or use the whip. *Maintain a firm seat.* Alternate squeezes and relaxation of the inside rein will lead the horse forward and support the inside leg. When you relax your inside hand, squeeze the outside rein in order to correct the bit (it often comes out more to the right) and lead the horse along the track of the circle. After a while, when he moves away from your leg, give him a sharp kick with your outside leg on the girth. Keep contact with your right rein. Continue the alternate squeezing and relaxing of your hands. Repeat the kick. Perhaps he will relax his neck and lower his head for a moment. When his head comes up again, repeat the kick, again with your outside leg. When he "gives in," start carefully at the trot, still on the circle a little on two tracks. The outside leg pushes him forward and reminds him every time he tries to raise his head. Ride some transitions to the walk, using mostly the inside rein, change the rein and ride him in the same way on the left rein. Finally, ride him on a figure of eight. Every time he resists, move him away from your inside leg and use the outside leg to bring him down.

The contact between the rider's leg and hands is also broken if the horse has developed the habit of being *behind the bit*. This bad habit is often hard to cure. That is why it is so important to prevent any tendency to drop the bit when training the young horse. He must be ridden forward and pushed into the bit with your legs and whip. The idea of the correction is to make him understand that he is never permitted to drop the bit. Ride him forward and shock him with a sharp kick with your outside leg on the girth, and move your outside hand forward at the same time. If his head comes up and he accepts the bit for a moment, your hands must be quiet. If he drops the bit again, repeat the procedure. Shock him with your voice when he drops the bit and reward him with your voice when he accepts it. When he starts to accept the bit, you can remind him with a short upward lift with one rein.

If a horse *refuses to turn,* he resists the inside aids, with the inside hind leg stuck to the ground. Tighten your seat, shorten your inside rein very much, lengthen the outside and move your inside hand strongly toward your hip, overbending the horse. By energetic use of your inside leg he will move and turn. As soon as he obeys, straighten him with the outside aids and push him forward in the new direction.

145

If a horse *presses against the wall,* save your outside leg from being squashed by raising your knee and moving your lower leg forward. Use the same aids as at the refusal to turn.

If a horse has a tendency to *buck,* take his head up and push forward. Be prepared if you feel a tension in the back and the horse moves with short, quick steps.

A horse can only *rear* from a standstill. It is therefore necessary to move him strongly forward and punish him with the whip at any tendency to rear. Take his head up. If he rears and you feel that he staggers, slip out of the irons and leave the horse. The bad habit of rearing should be cured by methodical suppling work. If the habit is deeply rooted, you can use the cavesson and punish him as soon as he rears.

If a horse *runs away,* you must take and give with your reins. Long hard pulls will make him go faster. Try to lead him with the rein on the soft side into a big circle, which you gradually diminish.

If a horse *shys,* he may be a little frightened or just mischievous. He turns his head toward the object. Remain calm and quietly show him the object. Next time you approach the object, bend him away from it and pass it at the shoulder-in.

There are minor bad habits. If the horse *tilts his head,* the ears not being at the same height, a short upward lift with one rein can be helpful.

146

Chapter VIII

THE COMPETITION

Going to a show gives you the opportunity of testing your standard and learning if you are on the right track in schooling your horse. It also gives you and your horse more experience. Perhaps you ride for fun, for the enjoyment of competing with other riders. Perhaps you ride to win. If you think the horse is ready for the particular test you intend to ride, you should do your utmost and ride to win.

Few riders will escape nervous tension before the competition, which, in the beginning, turns your legs to jelly and makes you think that the arena is the loneliest place in the world. You will get used to it, but to compete successfully you must be a little excited, the nerves, however, under control. A dull rider will never win.

Before you send in your entries, study the tests you plan to ride, and look carefully at the specific requirements of the tests to make sure that you are sufficiently trained for them.

School your horse in the various movements without regard to their sequence in any prescribed test. A horse should not be routined in a test. If he is, then he is likely to anticipate you and not yield himself completely to your will. A few days before the show, ride the test a sufficient number of times to assure yourself that you know it.

Memorize the test. Draw it on a paper, walk it in your room or outdoors. If you rely on the caller, you cannot concentrate on your ride or prepare the horse for the next movement, because you do not know what will happen at next marker. You can, of course, use the caller for safety's sake, but remember, if you aim high, then you must train to ride from memory.

If you plan to ride a Free Style test, you have to design an

147

LINDA ZANG   *Correct Turnout*

148

LINDA ZANG   *Correct Turnout—Full Dress*

149

artistic ride which includes movements appropriate to the level prescribed by the show management. Time allowed is specified in the Prize List. The rider is generally given a score (0-10) for artistic composition and one score for the execution (0-10). Sometimes, especially in the FEI levels, there is a list of numbered obligatory movements which are scored. Collective marks are also given as well as scores for artistic composition. A warning bell is rung one minute before the end of the time allowed.

When you design the Free Style test, think of symmetry (for instance, ride half-passes both ways), variations, riding the movements toward the judge as much as possible, and reaching a climax with the more demanding movements at the end of the test.

On the showground, try to make your horse familiar with the new surrounding. Ride him around the arena and expose him to the judge's stand, flags, flower pots, tents, colours.

Your greatest problem is to decide how much the horse should be worked before the test. Too much work will bring him under good control, but he will be tired and lose his brilliance. Too little work and he might be too "high." As horses are individuals, only experience will teach you. Inexperienced riders have a tendency to work their horses for hours and hours until the horse is dead tired and has lost all his brilliance. Most judges will prefer a gay, obedient horse (even if he makes some errors) to a tired, dull, obedient horse.

It is sometimes wise to give the horse fewer oats and, if necessary, no water before the competition.

If your horse is quiet, there is no reason to ride him more than 30 minutes before you start. The main purpose is to make him alert and responsive to your aids.*

Your first concern when you warm your horse up, must be to supple him and make him attentive to your aids, *not* to ride the movements of the test. When he is supple and you have established the degree of impulsion you want so that you can ride a smooth half-halt and extend without resistance or delay, then ride some movements of the test to control. It is too late to

* Should he need more work, you can ride him earlier in the day, several hours before the test, put him back in the stall and take him out again 30-45 minutes before you start.

school him now. There is no use throwing the yeast in the oven after the dough. Do not provoke big fights. After the warming up in connection with the test, dismount for a while, check the tack, clean your horse and his and your own equipment. Do not brood in a pessimistic way on the other competitors and their horses (always brilliant, obedient, supple with excellent paces). They feel the same way you do, but it is what *you* do that counts. It is a waste of time to think of them. Mount again about ten minutes before you start, and perhaps repeat the test in your mind. Repeat the *Three Pillars:*

1. Think and ride forward.
2. Ride your horse on the bit. Only exception free walk.
3. Maintain a correct and clock-even rhythm.

Now you are ready. Smile pleasantly and enter the arena. Good luck.

When riding tests, you and your horse should be turned out as well as possible. Do not overdo things, but try to emphasize your strong points and conceal your deficiencies. It is up to the judge to discover your weak points. If, in your opinion, you perform a movement badly, do not look desolate as if admitting the faultiness and making an excuse to the judge. Look instead a little nonchalant. Maybe it wasn't so bad, or the judge has a different opinion, or he didn't see it.

When you compete in dressage, you must be a bit of a philosopher. Don't complain after the ride: "he did so well at home!" Your horse, like yourself, has good days and less good days. If he is a horse of good standard and well trained, he should not have really bad days except for catastrophies. When both of you have a good day, you win, otherwise you are placed. Often if something goes wrong, the fault belongs with you and not with your horse. And don't complain about the scoring. The judges feel their responsibility and do their best. The easiest way to excuse mediocre performance is to blame the judge. Many riders talk about all the occasions when they were scored too low, but seldom or never talk about the occasions when they were scored too high. However, it all levels out in the long run.

151

APPENDIX

APPENDIX

THE SMALL ARENA

(20 x 40m)

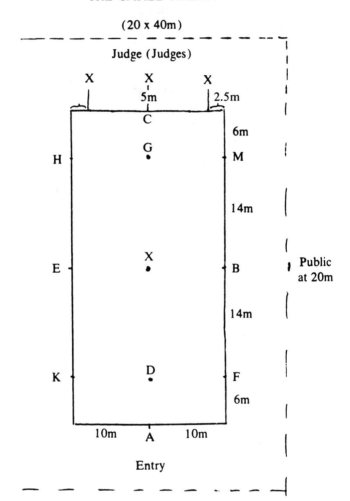

154

THE LARGE ARENA

(20 x 60m)

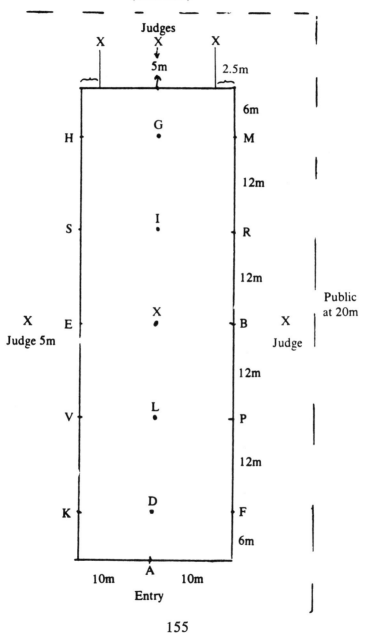

Judges

X   X   X

5m

2.5m

6m

G

H   M

12m

I

S   R

12m

X

X   E   B   X   Public
at 20m

Judge 5m   Judge

12m

L

V   P

12m

D

K   F

6m

10m   A   10m

Entry

155

SERPENTINE WITH SIX LOOPS

SERPENTINE WITH FOUR LOOPS

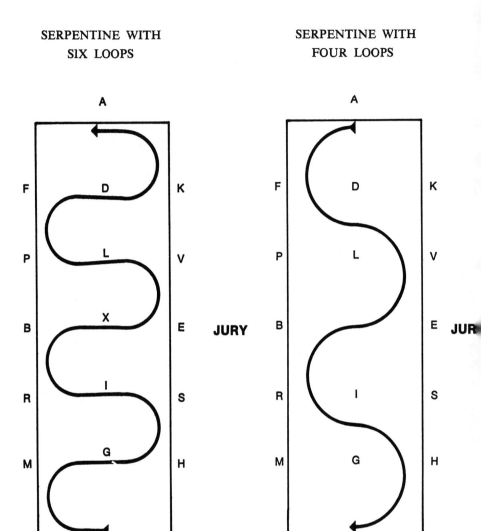

156

INDEX

INDEX

NOTES

NOTES

NOTES

NOTES